POSITIONS

JACQUES DERRIDA

Translated and Annotated by

Alan Bass

The University of Chicago Press

Originally published as *Positions,* © 1972 by Les Editions de Minuit.

The University of Chicago Press, Chicago 60637
The Athlone Press, London

© 1981 by The University of Chicago
All rights reserved. Published 1981
Paperback edition 1982
Printed in the United States of America
13 12 11 10 09 08 07   11 12 13 14

Library of Congress Cataloging-in-Publication Data

Derrida, Jacques.
  Positions.

  Translation of Positions.
  Interviews with Henri Ronse and others.
  1. Derrida, Jacques. I. Bass, Alan. II. Ronse,
Henri. III. Title.
B2430.D484D4713   194   80-17620
ISBN 0-226-14331-7 (paper)
This book is printed on acid-free paper.

CONTENTS

POSITIONS

NOTICE

These three interviews, the only ones in which I have
ever taken part, concern ongoing publications. Doubtless
they form—on the part of my interlocutors as on my
own—the gesture of an active interpretation. Determined
and dated, this is a reading of the work in which I find
myself *engaged:* which therefore is no more my own than
it remains arrested here. This too is a situation to be
read, a situation which has governed these exchanges in
their actuality, their content, and the form of their enunciations. Thus, no modifications were called for.

May 1972

IMPLICATIONS

Interview with
Henri Ronse

First published in *Lettres françaises* no. 1211, 6–12 December 1967.

Ronse: In a concluding note to *Writing and Difference* you stated: "what remains here the displacement of a question certainly forms a system." Is this not equally true for all your books? How are they organized?

Derrida: In effect they form, but indeed as a *displacement* and as the displacement of a *question,* a certain system somewhere open to an undecidable resource that sets the system in motion. The note to which you allude also recalled the necessity of those "blank spaces" which we know, at least since Mallarmé, "take on importance" in every text.

Ronse: And yet these books do not form a single Book...

Derrida: No. In what you call my books, what is first of all put in question is the unity of the book and the unity "book" considered as a perfect totality, with all the implications of such a concept. And you know that these implications concern the entirety of our culture, directly or indirectly. At the moment when such a closure *demarcates* itself, dare one maintain that one is the author of books, be they one, two, or three? Under these titles it is solely a question of a unique and differentiated textual "operation," if you will, whose unfinished movement assigns itself no absolute beginning, and which, although it is entirely consumed by the reading of other texts, in a certain fashion refers only to its own writing. We must adjust to conceiving these two contradictory ideas together. Therefore it would be impossible to provide a linear, deductive representation of these works that would correspond to some "logical order." Such an order is also in question, even if, I think, an entire phase or face of my texts conforms to its demands, at least by simulacrum, in order to inscribe it, in turn, into a composition that this order no longer governs. You know, in fact, that above all it is necessary to read and reread those in whose wake I write, the "books" in whose margins and between whose lines I mark out and read a text simultaneously almost identical and entirely other, that I would even hesitate, for obvious reasons, to call fragmentary . . .

Ronse: But *de facto,* if not *de jure,* where is one to make the first incision into such a reading?

Derrida: One can take *Of Grammatology* as a long essay articulated in two parts (whose juncture is not empirical, but theoretical, systematic) *into the middle* of which one could staple *Writing and Difference.*[1] *Grammatology* often calls upon it. In this case the interpretation of Rousseau would also be the twelfth "table" of the collection. Inversely, one could insert *Of Grammatology into the middle* of *Writing and Difference,* since six of the texts in that work preceded—*de facto* and *de jure*—the publication in *Critique* (two years ago) of the articles that announced *Of Grammatology;* the last five texts, beginning with "Freud and the Scene of Writing," are engaged in the grammatological opening. But things cannot be reconstituted so easily, as you may well imagine. In any case, that two "volumes" are to be inscribed one *in the middle of* the other is due, you will agree, to a strange geometry, of which these texts are doubtless the contemporaries.

Ronse: And *Speech and Phenomena?*[2]

Derrida: I forgot. It is perhaps the essay which I like most. Doubtless I could have bound it as a long note to one or the other of the other two works.[3] *Of Grammatol-*

ogy refers to it and economizes its development. But in a classical philosophical architecture, *Speech . . .* would come first: in it is posed, at a point which appears juridically decisive for reasons that I cannot explain here, the question of the privilege of the voice and of phonetic writing in their relationship to the entire history of the West, such as this history can be represented by the history of metaphysics, and metaphysics in its most modern, critical, and vigilant form: Husserl's transcendental phenomenology. What is "meaning," what are its historical relationships to what is purportedly identified under the rubric "voice" as a value of presence, presence of the object, presence of meaning to consciousness, self-presence in so called living speech and in self-consciousness? The essay which asks these questions can also be read as the other side (recto or verso, as you wish) of another essay, published in 1962, as the introduction to Husserl's *The Origin of Geometry*.[4] In this essay the problematic of writing was already in place as such, bound to the irreducible structure of "deferral" in its relationships to consciousness, presence, science, history and the history of science, the disappearance or delay of the origin, etc.

Ronse: I asked you where to begin, and you have led me into a labyrinth.

Derrida: All these texts, which are doubtless the interminable preface to another text that one day I would like to have the force to write, or still the epigraph to another that I would never have the audacity to write, are only the commentary on the sentence about a labyrinth of ciphers that is the epigraph to *Speech and Phenomena . . .*[5]

Ronse: This leads to a question one cannot avoid in reading you, in reading your privileged "examples" (Rousseau, Artaud, Bataille, Jabès). That is the question of the relationships between philosophy and non-philosophy. What is most striking from the outset is the difficulty of situating the style of your commentary. It seems to be almost impossible to define the status of your discourse. But is it necessary to try to do so? Doesn't this question itself fall within the realm of metaphysics?

Derrida: I try to keep myself at the *limit* of philosophical discourse. I say limit and not death, for I do not at all believe in what today is so easily called the death of philosophy (nor, moreover, in the simple death of whatever—the book, man, or god, especially since, as we all know, what is dead wields a very specific power). Thus, the limit on the basis of which philosophy became possible, defined itself as the *epistēmē*, functioning within a system of fundamental constraints, conceptual oppositions outside of which philosophy becomes impracticable. In my readings, I try therefore, by means of a necessarily double gesture . . .

Ronse: You say in your Freud[6] that one writes with two hands . . .

Derrida: Yes, by means of this double play, marked in certain decisive places by an erasure which allows what it obliterates to be read, violently inscribing within the text that which attempted to govern it from without, I try to respect as rigorously as possible the internal, regulated play of philosophemes or epistimemes by making them slide—without mistreating them—to the point of their nonpertinence, their exhaustion, their closure. To "deconstruct" philosophy, thus, would be to think—in the most faithful, interior way—the structured genealogy of philosophy's concepts, but at the same time to determine—from a certain exterior that is unqualifiable or unnameable by philosophy—what this history has been able to dissimulate or forbid, making itself into a history by means of this somewhere motivated repression. By means of this simultaneously faithful and violent circulation between the inside and the outside of philosophy—that is of the West—there is produced a certain textual work that gives great pleasure. That is, a writing interested in itself which also enables us to read philosophemes—and consequently all the texts of our culture—as kinds of symptoms (a word which I suspect, of course, as I explain elsewhere) of something that *could not be presented* in the history of philosophy, and which, moreover, is *nowhere present*, since all of this concerns putting into question the major determination of the meaning of Being[7] as *presence*, the determination in which Heidegger recognized the destiny of philosophy. Now, one can follow the treatment accorded to writing as a particularly revelatory symptom, from Plato to Rousseau, Saussure, Husserl, occasionally Heidegger himself, and *a fortiori* in all the modern discourses—sometimes the most faithful ones—that remain within Husserl's and Heidegger's questions. Such a symptom is necessarily, and structurally, dissimulated, for reasons and along pathways that I attempt to analyze. And if this symptom is revealed today, it is not at all due to some more or less ingenious discovery initiated by someone here or there. It is due rather to a certain total transformation (that can no longer even be called "historical" or "worldwide," because the transformation infringes upon the security of such significations) that also can be ascertained in other determined fields (mathematical and logical formalization, linguistics, ethnology, psychoanalysis, political economy, biology, the technology of information, programming, etc.).

Ronse: In your essays at least two meanings of the word "writing" are discernible: the accepted meaning, which opposes (phonetic) writing to the speech that it allegedly represents (but you show that there is no purely phonetic writing), and a more radical meaning that determines writing in general, before any tie to what glossematics[8] calls an "expressive substance"; this more radical meaning would be the common root of writing and speech.

The treatment accorded to writing in the accepted sense serves as a revelatory index of the repression to which archi-writing is subject. An inevitable repression whose necessity, forms, and laws are to be investigated. This (archi-) writing is linked to a chain of other names: archi-trace, reserve, articulation, *brisure*,⁹ supplement, and *différance*.¹⁰ Much has been said above about the *a* of *différance*. What does it signify?

Derrida: I do not know if it *signifies* at all—perhaps something like the production of what metaphysics calls the sign (signified/signifier). You have noticed that this *a* is written or read, but cannot be heard. And first off I insist upon the fact that any discourse—for example, ours, at this moment—on this alteration, this graphic and grammatical aggression, implies an irreducible reference to the mute intervention of a written sign. The present participle of the verb *différer,* on which this noun is modeled, ties together a configuration of concepts I hold to be systematic and irreducible, each one of which intervenes, or rather is accentuated, at a decisive moment of the work. *First, différance* refers to the (active *and* passive) movement that consists in deferring by means of delay, delegation, reprieve, referral, detour, postponement, reserving. In this sense, *différance* is not preceded by the originary and indivisible unity of a present possibility that I could reserve, like an expenditure that I would put off calculatedly or for reasons of economy. What defers presence, on the contrary, is the very basis on which presence is announced or desired in what represents it, its sign, its trace . . .

Ronse: From this point of view *différance* is an economical question?

Derrida: I would even say that it is *the* economical concept, and since there is no economy without *différance*, it is the most general structure of economy, given that one understands by economy something other than the classical economy of metaphysics, or the classical metaphysics of economy. *Second*, the movement of *dif-férance*, as that which produces different things, that which differentiates, is the common root of all the oppo-sitional concepts that mark our language, such as, to take only a few examples, sensible/intelligible, intuition/signification, nature/culture, etc. As a common root, *différance* is also the element of the *same* (to be distin-guished from the identical) in which these oppositions are announced. *Third, différance* is also the production, if it can still be put this way, of these differences, of the diacriticity that the linguistics generated by Saussure, and all the structural sciences modeled upon it, have re-called is the condition for any signification and any structure. These differences—and, for example, the taxonomical science which they may occasion—are the effects of *différance;* they are neither inscribed in the heavens, nor in the brain, which does not mean that they are produced by the activity of some speaking subject. From this point of view, the concept of *différance* is neither simply structuralist, nor simply geneticist,[11] such an alternative itself being an "effect" of *différance.* I would even say, but perhaps we will come to this later, that it is not simply a concept . . .

Ronse: I also have been struck that already in your essay on "Force and Signification" *différance* (but you did not yet call it that)[12] led you back to Nietzsche (who linked the concept of force to the irreducibility of dif-ferences), and later to Freud, all of whose opposed con-cepts you showed to be governed by the economy of *différance,* and finally, always, above all, to Heidegger.

Derrida: Yes, above all. What I have attempted to do would not have been possible without the opening of Heidegger's questions. And first, since we must proceed rapidly here, would not have been possible without the attention to what Heidegger calls the difference between Being and beings, the ontico-ontological difference such as, in a way, it remains unthought by philosophy. But

despite this debt to Heidegger's thought, or rather because of it, I attempt to locate in Heidegger's text—
which, no more than any other, is not homogeneous,
continuous, everywhere equal to the greatest force and
to all the consequences of its questions—the signs of a
belonging to metaphysics, or to what he calls onto-
theology. Moreover, Heidegger recognizes that econom-
ically and strategically he had to borrow the syntaxic and
lexical resources of the language of metaphysics, as one
always must do at the very moment that one deconstructs
this language. Therefore we must work to locate these
metaphysical holds, and to reorganize unceasingly the
form and sites of our questioning. Now, among these
holds, the ultimate determination of difference as the
ontico-ontological difference—however necessary and
decisive this phase may be—still seems to me, in a
strange way, to be in the grasp of metaphysics. Perhaps
then, moving along lines that would be more Nietz-
schean than Heideggerean, by going to the end of this
thought of the truth of Being, we would have to become
open to a *différance* that is no longer determined, in the
language of the West, as the difference between Being
and beings. Such a departure is doubtless not possible
today, but one could show how it is in preparation. In
Heidegger, first of all. *Différance—fourth—*therefore
would name provisionally this unfolding of difference,
in particular, but not only, or first of all, of the ontico-
ontological difference.

  Ronse: Does not the limit of which you are speaking,
communicate, in Heidegger, as you sometimes seem to
suggest, with a certain "phonologism"?

  Derrida: It is not a question of a limit, or, in any event,
like every limit it ensures power and grasp, and here it is
of an unreplaceable force. But doubtless there is a certain
Heideggerean phonologism, a noncritical privilege accorded in his works, as in the West in general, to the
voice, to a determined "expressive substance." This

privilege, whose consequences are considerable and systematic, can be recognized, for example, in the significant prevalence of so many "phonic" metaphors in a meditation on art which always returns, by means of examples chosen in a very marked way, to art as the "appearance of truth." Now, the admirable meditation by means of which Heidegger repeats the origin or essence of truth never puts into question the link to logos and to *phonē*. Thus is explained that according to Heidegger all the arts unfold in the space of the poem which is "the essence of art," in the space of "language," and of the "word." "Architecture and sculpture," he says, "occur only in the opening of saying and naming. They are governed and guided by them." Thus is explained the privilege accorded, in a very classical fashion, to poetic speech *(Dichtung)* and to song, and the disdain for literature. Heidegger says that *Dichtung* must be liberated from literature, etc.

Ronse: This last remark is indicative of the attention you constantly bring to bear on a certain irreducibility of writing or of "literary" spacing. It is here that your works often seem affiliated with those of the *Tel Quel* group.[13]

Derrida: I can say in any event that what is at stake in the current research of this group, as in any analogous research, seems to me extremely important, important in a way measured less well in France, it appears, than abroad, and, significantly, less well in the West than in certain Eastern countries. If we had the time, we could analyze the reasons why, and ask ourselves too, why the irreducibility of writing and, let us say, the subversion of logocentrism are announced better than elsewhere, today, in a certain sector and certain determined form of "literary" practice. But you can very well understand why I would write this word between quotation marks, and what equivocality must be brought into play. This new practice supposes a break with what has tied the history of the literary arts to the history of metaphysics . . .

Ronse: Can there be a surpassing of this metaphysics? Can a graphocentrism be opposed to a logocentrism? Can there be an effective transgression of closure, and what then would be the conditions for a transgressive discourse?

Derrida: There *is not* a transgression, if one understands by that a pure and simple landing into a beyond of metaphysics, at a point which also would be, let us not forget, first of all a point of language or writing. Now, even in aggressions or transgressions, we are consorting with a code to which metaphysics is tied irreducibly, such that every transgressive gesture reencloses us—precisely by giving us a hold on the closure of metaphysics— within this closure. But, by means of the work done on one side and the other of the limit the field inside is modified, and a transgression is produced that consequently is nowhere present as a *fait accompli.* One is never installed within transgression, one never lives elsewhere. Transgression implies that the limit is always at work. Now, the "thought-that-means-nothing," the thought that exceeds meaning and meaning-as-hearing-oneself-speak by interrogating them—this thought, announced in grammatology, is given precisely as the thought for which there is no sure opposition between outside and inside. At the conclusion of a certain work, even the concepts of excess or of transgression can become suspect.

This is why it has never been a question of opposing a graphocentrism to a logocentrism, nor, in general, any center to any other center. *Of Grammatology* is not a defense and illustration of grammatology. And even less a rehabilitation of what has always been called writing. It is not a question of returning to writing its rights, its superiority or its dignity. Plato said of writing that it was an orphan or a bastard, as opposed to speech, the legitimate and high-born son of the "father of logos."[14] At the moment when one attempts to interrogate this family scene, and to investigate all the investments, ethical and otherwise, of this entire history, nothing would be more ridiculously mystifying than such an ethical or axiological reversal, returning a prerogative or some elder's right to writing. I believe that I have explained myself clearly on this subject. *Of Grammatology* is the title of a question: a question about the necessity of a science of writing, about the conditions that would make it possible, about the critical work that would have to open its field and resolve the epistemological obstacles; but it is also a question about the limits of this science. And these limits, on which I have insisted no less, are also those of the classical notion of science, whose projects, concepts, and norms are fundamentally and systematically tied to metaphysics.

Ronse: It is in this sense that the idea of the end of the book and the beginning of writing that you invoke in *Of Grammatology* should be read. It is not a positive or sociological statement.

Derrida: Perhaps it is that too, very secondarily. A place is made, in that essay, by all rights, for such a positive inquiry into the current upheavals in the forms of communication, the new structures emerging in all the formal practices, and also in the domains of the archive and the treatment of information, that massively and systematically reduce the role of speech, of phonetic writing, and of the book. But one would be mistaken in coming to the conclusion of a death of the book and a birth of writing from that which is entitled "The End of the Book and the Beginning of Writing." One page before the chapter which bears this title a distinction is proposed between *closure* and *end*. What is held within the demarcated closure may continue indefinitely. If one does not simply read the title, it announces precisely that there is no end of the book and no beginning of writing. The chapter shows just that: writing does not begin. It is even on the basis of writing, if it can be put this way, that one can put into question the search for an *archie,* an absolute beginning, an origin. Writing can no more begin, therefore, than the book can end . . .

Ronse: This properly *infinite* movement might be a little bit like the patient metaphor for your work.

Derrida: I try to *write* (in) the space in which is posed the question of speech and meaning. I try to write the question: (what is) meaning to say?[15] Therefore it is necessary in such a space, and guided by such a question, that writing literally mean nothing. Not that it is absurd in the way that absurdity has always been in solidarity with metaphysical meaning. It simply tempts itself, tenders itself, attempts to keep itself at the point of the exhaustion of meaning. To risk meaning nothing is to start to play, and first to enter into the play of *différance* which prevents any word, any concept, any major enunciation from coming to summarize and to govern from the theological presence of a center the movement and textual spacing of differences. Whence, for example, the chain of substitutions of which you were speaking a while ago (archi-trace, archi-writing, reserve, *brisure,* articulation, supplement, *différance;* there will be others) which is not simply a metonymical operation that would leave intact the conceptual identities, the signified idealities, that the chain would be happy just to translate, to put in circulation. It is in this sense that I risk meaning nothing that can simply be heard, or that is a simple affair of hearing. To be entangled in hundreds of pages of a writing simultaneously insistent and elliptical, imprinting, as you saw, even its erasures, carrying off each concept into an interminable chain of differences, surrounding or confusing itself with so many precautions, references, notes, citations, collages, supplements—this "meaning-to-say-nothing" is not, you will agree, the most assured of exercises.

SEMIOLOGY
AND
GRAMMATOLOGY
Interview with
Julia Kristeva

First published in *Information sur les sciences sociales* 7, 3 June 1968.

Kristeva: Semiology today is constructed on the model of the sign and its correlates: *communication* and *structure.* What are the "logocentric" and ethnocentric limits of these models, and how are they incapable of serving as the basis for a notation attempting to escape metaphysics?

Derrida: All gestures here are necessarily equivocal. And supposing, which I do not believe, that someday it will be possible *simply* to escape metaphysics, the concept of the sign will have marked, in this sense, a simultaneous impediment and progress. For if the sign, by its root and its implications, is in all its aspects metaphysical, if it is in systematic solidarity with stoic and medieval theology, the work and the displacement to which it has been submitted—and of which it also, curiously, is the instrument—have had *delimiting* effects. For this work and displacement have permitted the critique of how the concept of the sign belongs to metaphysics, which represents a simultaneous *marking* and *loosening* of the limits of the system in which this concept was born and began to serve, and thereby also represents, to a certain extent, an uprooting of the sign from its own soil. This work must be conducted as far as possible, but at a certain point one inevitably encounters "the logocentric and ethnocentric limits" of such a model. At this point, perhaps, the concept is to be abandoned. But this point is very difficult to determine, and is never pure. All the heuristic and critical resources of the concept of the sign have to be exhausted, and exhausted equally in all domains and contexts. Now, it is inevitable that not only inequalities of development (which will always occur), but also the necessity of certain contexts, will render strategically indispensable the recourse to a model known elsewhere, and even at the most novel points of investigation, to function as an obstacle.

To take only one example, one could show that a **semiology of the Saussurean type has had a double role.** *On the one hand,* an absolutely decisive critical role:

1. It has marked, against the tradition, that the signified is inseparable from the signifier, that the signified and signifier are the two sides of one and the same production. Saussure even purposely refused to have this opposition or this "two-sided unity" conform to the relationship between soul and body, as had always been done. "This two-sided unity has often been compared to the unity of the human person, composed of a body and a soul. The comparison is hardly satisfactory." (*Cours de linguistique générale*, p. 145)

2. By emphasizing the *differential* and *formal* characteristics of semiological functioning, by showing that it "is impossible for sound, the material element, itself to belong to language" and that "in its essence it [the linguistic signifier] is not at all phonic" (p. 164); by desubstantializing both the signified content and the "expressive substance"—which therefore is no longer in a privileged or exclusive way phonic—by making linguistics a division of general semiology (p. 33), Saussure powerfully contributed to turning against the metaphysical tradition the concept of the sign that he borrowed from it.

And yet Saussure could not not confirm this tradition in the extent to which he continued to use the concept of the sign. No more than any other, this concept cannot be employed in both an absolutely novel and an absolutely conventional way. One necessarily assumes, in a non-critical way, at least some of the implications inscribed in its system. There is at least one moment at which Saussure must renounce drawing all the conclusions from the critical work he has undertaken, and that is the not for-tuitous moment when he resigns himself to using the word "sign," lacking anything better. After having jus-tified the introduction of the words "signified" and "sig-nifier," Saussure writes: "As for *sign*, if we retain it, it is because we find nothing else to replace it, everyday lan-guage suggesting no other" (pp. 99–100). And, in effect, it is difficult to see how one could evacuate the *sign* when one has begun by proposing the opposition signified/signifier.

Now, "everyday language" is not innocent or neutral. It is the language of Western metaphysics, and it carries with it not only a considerable number of presupposi-tions of all types, but also presuppositions inseparable from metaphysics, which, although little attended to, are knotted into a system. This is why *on the other hand:*

1. The maintenance of the rigorous distinction—an essential and juridical distinction—between the *signans* and the *signatum*, the equation of the *signatum* and the concept (p. 99),[1] inherently leaves open the possibility of thinking a *concept signified in and of itself,* a concept sim-ply present for thought, independent of a relationship to language, that is of a relationship to a system of sig-nifiers. By leaving open this possibility—and it is inher-ent even in the opposition signifier/signified, that is in the sign—Saussure contradicts the critical acquisitions of which we were just speaking. He accedes to the classical exigency of what I have proposed to call a "transcenden-tal signified," which in and of itself, in its essence, would refer to no signifier, would exceed the chain of

signs, and would no longer itself function as a signifier. On the contrary, though, from the moment that one questions the possibility of such a transcendental signified, and that one recognizes that every signified is also in the position of a signifier,[2] the distinction between signified and signifier becomes problematical at its root. Of course this is an operation that must be undertaken with prudence for: (a) it must pass through the difficult deconstruction of the entire history of metaphysics which imposed, and never will cease to impose upon semiological science in its entirety this fundamental quest for a "transcendental signified" and a concept independent of language; this quest not being imposed from without by something like "philosophy," but rather by everything that links our language, our culture, our "system of thought" to the history and system of metaphysics; (b) nor is it a question of confusing at every level, and in all simplicity, the signifier and the signified. That this opposition or difference cannot be radical or absolute does not prevent it from functioning, and even from being indispensable within certain limits—very wide limits. For example, no translation would be possible without it. In effect, the theme of a transcendental signified took shape within the horizon of an absolutely pure, transparent, and unequivocal translatability. In the limits to which it is possible, or at least *appears* possible, translation practices the difference between signified and signifier. But if this difference is never pure, no more so is translation, and for the notion of translation we would have to substitute a notion of *transformation:* a regulated transformation of one language by another, of one text by another. We will never have, and in fact have never had, to do with some "transport" of pure signifieds from one language to another, or within one and the same language, that the signifying instrument would leave virgin and untouched.

2. Although he recognized the necessity of putting the phonic substance between brackets ("What is essential in language, we shall see, is foreign to the phonic character of the linguistic sign" [p. 21]. "In its essence it [the linguistic signifier] is not at all phonic" [p. 164]), Saussure, for essential, and essentially metaphysical, reasons had to privilege speech, everything that links the sign to *phonē*. He also speaks of the "natural link" between thought and voice, meaning and sound (p. 46). He even speaks of "thought-sound" (p. 156). I have attempted elsewhere to show what is traditional in such a gesture, and to what necessities it submits. In any event, it winds up contradicting the most interesting critical motive of the *Course*, making of linguistics the regulatory model, the "pattern" for a general semiology of which it was to be, by all rights and theoretically, only a part. The theme of the arbitrary, thus, is turned away from its most fruitful paths (formalization) toward a hierarchizing teleology: "Thus it can be said that entirely arbitrary signs realize better than any others the ideal of the semiological process; this is why language, the most complex and most widespread of the systems of expression, is also the most characteristic one of them all; in this sense linguistics can become the *general pattern for all semiology,* even though language is only a particular system" (p. 101). One finds exactly the same gesture and the same concepts in Hegel. The contradiction between these two moments of the *Course* is also marked by Saussure's recognizing elsewhere that "it is not spoken language that is natural to man, but the faculty of constituting a language, that is, a system of distinct signs . . . ," that is, the possibility of the *code* and of *articulation,* independent of any substance, for example, phonic substance.

3. The concept of the sign (signifier/signified) carries within itself the necessity of privileging the phonic substance and of setting up linguistics as the "pattern" for

semiology. *Phonē*, in effect, is the signifying substance *given to consciousness* as that which is most intimately tied to the thought of the signified concept. From this point of view, the voice is consciousness itself. When I speak, not only am I conscious of being present for what I think, but I am conscious also of keeping as close as possible to my thought, or to the "concept," a signifier that does not fall into the world, a signifier that I hear as soon as I emit it, that seems to depend upon my pure and free spontaneity, requiring the use of no instrument, no accessory, no force taken from the world. Not only do the signifier and the signified seem to unite, but also, in this confusion, the signifier seems to erase itself or to become transparent, in order to allow the concept to present itself as what it is, referring to nothing other than its presence. The exteriority of the signifier seems reduced. Naturally this experience is a lure, but a lure whose necessity has organized an entire structure, or an entire epoch; and on the grounds of this epoch a semiology has been constituted whose concepts and fundamental presuppositions are quite precisely discernible from Plato to Husserl, passing through Aristotle, Rousseau, Hegel, etc.

4. To reduce the exteriority of the signifier is to exclude everything in semiotic practice that is not psychic. Now, only the privilege accorded to the phonetic and linguistic sign can authorize Saussure's proposition according to which the "linguistic sign is therefore a two-sided *psychic* entity" (p. 99). Supposing that this proposition has a rigorous sense in and of itself, it is difficult to see how it could be extended to every sign, be it phonetic-linguistic or not. It is difficult to see therefore, except, precisely, by making of the phonetic sign the "pattern" for all signs, how general semiology can be inscribed in a psychology. However, this is what Saussure does: "One can thus conceive of a science that would study the life of signs at the heart of social life; it would form a part of social psychol-

ogy, and consequently of general psychology; we will name it semiology (from the Greek *sēmeion*, 'sign'). It would teach what signs consist of, what laws regulate them. Since it does not yet exist, one cannot say what it will be; but it has a right to exist, its place is determined in advance. Linguistics is only a part of this general science, the laws that semiology will discover will be applicable to linguistics, and the latter will find itself attached to a well defined domain in the set of human facts. It is for the psychologist to determine the exact place of semiology" (p. 33).

Of course modern linguists and semioticians have not remained with Saussure, or at least with this Saussurean "psychologism." The Copenhagen School and all of American linguistics have explicitly criticized it. But if I have insisted on Saussure, it is not only because even those who criticize him recognize him as the founder of general semiology and borrow most of their concepts from him; but above all because one cannot simply criticize the "psychologistic" usage of the concept of the sign. Psychologism is not the poor usage of a good concept, but is inscribed and prescribed within the concept of the sign itself, in the equivocal manner of which I spoke at the beginning. This equivocality, which weighs upon the model of the sign, marks the "semiological" project itself and the organic totality of its concepts, in particular that of *communication,* which in effect implies a *transmission charged with making pass, from one subject to another, the identity* of a *signified* object, of a *meaning* or of a *concept* rightfully separable from the process of passage and from the signifying operation. Communication presupposes subjects (whose identity and presence are constituted before the signifying operation) and objects (signified concepts, a thought meaning that the passage of communication will have neither to constitute, nor, by all rights, to transform). *A* communicates *B* to *C*. Through the sign the emitter communicates something to a receptor, etc.

The case of the concept of *structure*, that you also bring up, is certainly more ambiguous. Everything depends upon how one sets it to work. Like the concept of the sign—and therefore of semiology—it can simultaneously confirm and shake logocentric and ethnocentric assuredness. It is not a question of junking these concepts, nor do we have the means to do so. Doubtless it is more necessary, from within semiology, to transform concepts, to displace them, to turn them against their presuppositions, to reinscribe them in other chains, and little by little to modify the terrain of our work and thereby produce new configurations; I do not believe in decisive ruptures, in an unequivocal "epistemological break," as it is called today. Breaks are always, and fatally, reinscribed in an old cloth that must continually, interminably be undone. This interminability is not an accident or contingency; it is essential, systematic, and theoretical. And this in no way minimizes the necessity and relative importance of certain breaks, of the appearance and definition of new structures . . .

Kristeva: What is the *gram* as a "new structure of nonpresence"? What is *writing* as *différance*? What rupture do these concepts introduce in relation to the key concepts of semiology—the (phonetic) *sign* and *structure*? How does the notion of *text* replace, in grammatology, the linguistic and semiological notion of what is *enounced*?

Derrida: The reduction of writing—as the reduction of the exteriority of the signifier—was part and parcel of phonologism and logocentrism. We know how Saussure, according to the traditional operation that was also Plato's, Aristotle's, Rousseau's, Hegel's, Husserl's, etc., excludes writing from the field of linguistics—from language and speech—as a phenomenon of exterior representation, both useless and dangerous: "The linguistic object is not defined by the combination of the written word and the spoken word, the latter alone constituting this object" (p. 45); "writing is foreign to the internal system [of language]" (p. 44); "writing veils our view of language: it does not clothe language, but travesties it" (p. 51). The tie of writing to language is "superficial," "factitious." It is "bizarre" that writing, which should only be an "image," "usurps the principal role" and that "the natural relationship is inversed" (p. 47). Writing is a "trap," its action is "vicious" and "tyrannical," its misdeeds are monstrosities, "teratological cases," "linguistics should put them under observation in a special compartment" (p. 54), etc. Naturally, this representativist conception of writing ("Language and writing are two distinct sign systems; the unique *raison d'être* of the second is to *represent* the first" [p. 45]) is linked to the practice of phonetic-alphabetic writing, to which Saussure realizes his study is "limited" (p. 48). In effect, alphabetical writing seems to present speech, and at the same time to erase itself before speech. Actually, it could be shown, as I have attempted to do, that there is no purely phonetic writing, and that phonologism is less a consequence of the practice of the alphabet in a given culture than a certain ethical or axiological *experience* of this practice. Writing *should* erase itself before the plenitude of living speech, perfectly represented in the transparence of its notation, immediately present for the subject who speaks it, and for the subject who receives its meaning, content, value.

Now, if one ceases to limit oneself to the model of phonetic writing, which we privilege only by ethnocentrism, and if we draw all the consequences from the fact that there is no purely phonetic writing (by reason of the necessary spacing of signs, punctuation, intervals, the differences indispensable for the functioning of graphemes, etc.), then the entire phonologist or logocentrist logic becomes problematical. Its range of legitimacy becomes narrow and superficial. This delimitation, however, is indispensable if one wants to be able to account, with some coherence, for the principle of difference, such as Saussure himself recalls it. This principle compels us not only not to privilege one substance—here the phonic, so called temporal, substance—while excluding another—for example, the graphic, so called spatial, substance—but even to consider every process of signification as a formal play of differences. That is, of traces.

Why traces? And by what right do we reintroduce grammatics at the moment when we seem to have neutralized every substance, be it phonic, graphic, or otherwise? Of course it is not a question of resorting to the same concept of writing and of simply inverting the dissymmetry that now has become problematical. It is a question, rather, of producing a new concept of writing. This concept can be called *gram* or *différance*. The play of differences supposes, in effect, syntheses and referrals which forbid at any moment, or in any sense, that a simple element be *present* in and of itself, referring only to itself. Whether in the order of spoken or written discourse, no element can function as a sign without referring to another element which itself is not simply present. This interweaving results in each "element"—phoneme or grapheme—being constituted on the basis of the trace within it of the other elements of the chain or system. This interweaving, this textile, is the *text* produced only in the transformation of another text. Nothing, neither among the elements nor within the system, is anywhere ever simply present or absent. There are only, everywhere, differences and traces of traces. The gram, then, is the most general concept of semiology—which thus becomes grammatology—and it covers not only the field of writing in the restricted sense, but also the field of linguistics. The advantage of this concept—provided that it be surrounded by a certain interpretive context, for no more than any other conceptual element it does not signify, or suffice, by itself—is that in principle it neutralizes the phonologistic propensity of the "sign," and *in fact counterbalances* it by liberating the entire scientific field of the "graphic substance" (history and systems of writing beyond the bounds of the West) whose interest is not minimal, but which so far has been left in the shadows of neglect.

The gram as *différance*, then, is a structure and a movement no longer conceivable on the basis of the opposition presence/absence. *Différance* is the systematic play of differences, of the traces of differences, of the *spacing* by means of which elements are related to each other. This spacing is the simultaneously active and passive (the *a* of *différance* indicates this indecision as concerns activity and passivity, that which cannot be governed by or distributed between the terms of this opposition)[3] production of the intervals without which the "full" terms would not signify, would not function. It is also the becoming-space of the spoken chain—which has been called temporal or linear; a becoming-space which makes possible both writing and every correspondence between speech and writing, every passage from one to the other.

The activity or productivity connoted by the *a* of *différance* refers to the generative movement in the play of differences. The latter are neither fallen from the sky nor inscribed once and for all in a closed system, a static structure that a synchronic and taxonomic operation could exhaust. Differences are the effects of transformations, and from this vantage the theme of *différance* is incompatible with the static, synchronic, taxonomic, ahistoric motifs in the concept of *structure*. But it goes without saying that this motif is not the only one that

defines structure, and that the production of differences,
différance, is not astructural: it produces systematic and
regulated transformations which are able, at a certain
point, to leave room for a structural science. The concept
of *différance* even develops the most legitimate principled
exigencies of "structuralism."

Language, and in general every semiotic code—which
Saussure defines as "classifications"—are therefore effects, but their cause is not a subject, a substance, or a
being somewhere present and outside the movement of
différance. Since there is no presence before and outside
semiological *différance*, one can extend to the system of
signs in general what Saussure says of language: "Language is necessary for speech to be intelligible and to
produce all its effects; but speech is necessary for language to be established; historically, the fact of speech
always comes first." There is a circle here, for if one
rigorously distinguishes language and speech, code and
message, schema and usage, etc., and if one wishes to do
justice to the two postulates thus enunciated, one does
not know where to begin, nor how something can begin
in general, be it language or speech. Therefore, one has
to admit, before any dissociation of language and speech,
code and message, etc. (and everything that goes along
with such a dissociation), a systematic production of differences, the *production* of a system of differences—a
différance—within whose effects one eventually, by
abstraction and according to determined motivations,
will be able to demarcate a linguistics of language and a
linguistics of speech, etc.

Nothing—no present and in-*different* being—thus
precedes *différance* and spacing. There is no subject who
is agent, author, and master of *différance*, who eventually
and empirically would be overtaken by *différance*.
Subjectivity—like objectivity—is an effect of *différance*,
an effect inscribed in a system of *différance*. This is why
the *a* of *différance* also recalls that spacing is temporiza-

tion, the detour and postponement by means of which intuition, perception, consummation—in a word, the relationship to the present, the reference to a present reality, to a *being*—are always *deferred*. Deferred by virtue of the very principle of difference which holds that an element functions and signifies, takes on or conveys meaning, only by referring to another past or future element in an economy of traces. This economic aspect of *différance*, which brings into play a certain not conscious calculation in a field of forces, is inseparable from the more narrowly semiotic aspect of *différance*. It confirms that the subject, and first of all the conscious and speaking subject, depends upon the system of differences and the movement of *différance*, that the subject is not present, nor above all present to itself before *différance*, that the subject is constituted only in being divided from itself, in becoming space, in temporizing, in deferral; and it confirms that, as Saussure said, "language [which consists only of differences] is not a function of the speaking subject." At the point at which the concept of *différance*, and the chain attached to it, intervenes, all the conceptual oppositions of metaphysics (signifier/signified; sensible/intelligible; writing/speech; passivity/activity; etc.)—to the extent that they ultimately refer to the presence of something present (for example, in the form of the identity of the subject who is present for all his operations, present beneath every accident or event, self-present in its "living speech," in its enunciations, in the present objects and acts of its language, etc.)—become nonpertinent. They all amount, at one moment or another, to a subordination of the movement of *différance* in favor of the presence of a value or a *meaning* supposedly antecedent to *différance*, more original than it, exceeding and governing it in the last analysis. This is still the presence of what we called above the "transcendental signified."

Kristeva: It is said that the concept of "meaning" in semiotics is markedly different from the phenomenological concept of "meaning." In what ways, however, are they complicit, and to what extent does the semiological project remain intrametaphysical?

Derrida: It is true that at first the phenomenological extension of the concept of "meaning" appears much wider, much less determined. All experience is the experience of meaning *(Sinn)*. Everything that appears to consciousness, everything that is for consciousness in general, is *meaning*. Meaning is the phenomenality of the phenomenon. In the *Logical Researches* Husserl rejected Frege's distinction between *Sinn* and *Bedeutung*. Later this distinction seemed useful to him, not that he understood it as did Frege, but in order to mark the dividing line between meaning in its most general extension *(Sinn)* and meaning as an object of logical or linguistic enunciation, meaning as signification *(Bedeutung)*. It is at this point that the complicity to which you allude may appear. Thus, for example:

1. Husserl, in order to isolate meaning *(Sinn* or *Bedeutung)* from enunciation or from the intention of signification *(Bedeutungs-intention)* that "animates" enunciation, needs to distinguish rigorously between the signifying (sensible) aspect, whose originality he recognizes, but which he excludes from his logico-grammatical problematic, and the aspect of signified meaning (which is intelligible, ideal, "spiritual"). Perhaps we had best cite a passage from *Ideas* here:

> Let us start from the familiar distinction between the sensory, the so to speak bodily aspect of expression, and its nonsensory "mental" aspect. There is no need for us to enter more closely into the discussion of the first aspect, nor upon the way of uniting the two aspects, though we clearly have title-headings here indicated for phenomenological problems that are not unimportant. We restrict our glance exclusively to "meaning" [*Bedeutung*], and "meaning something" [*Bedeuten*]. Originally these words relate only to the

sphere of speech [*sprachliche Sphäre*], that of "expression" [*des Ausdruckens*]. But it is almost inevitable, and
at the same time an important step for knowledge, to
extend the meaning of these words, and to modify
them suitably so that they may be applied in a certain
way to the whole noetico-noematic sphere, to all acts,
therefore, whether these are interwoven [*verflochten*]
with expression acts or not. With this in view we ourselves, when referring to any intentional experiences,
have spoken all along of *"Sinn"* [sense], a word which
is generally used as an equivalent for *"Bedeutung"*
[meaning]. We propose in the interests of distinctness
to favour the word *Bedeutung* (meaning at the conceptual level) when referring to the old concept, and
more particularly in the complex speech-form *"logical"*
or *"expressing" meaning*. We use the word *Sinn* [sense
or meaning *simpliciter*] in the future, as before, in its
more embracing breadth of applications.[4]

Thus, whether or not it is "signified" or "expressed,"
whether or not it is "interwoven" with a process of signification, "meaning" is an intelligible or spiritual
ideality which eventually can be united to the sensible
aspect of a signifier that in itself it does not need. Its
presence, meaning, or essence of meaning, is conceivable outside this interweaving as soon as the
phenomenologist, like the semiotician, allegedly refers to
a pure unity, a rigorously identifiable aspect of meaning
or of the signified.

2. This layer of pure meaning, or a pure signified,
refers, explicitly in Husserl and at least implicitly in
semiotic practice, to a layer of prelinguistic or presemi-
otic (preexpressive, Husserl calls it) meaning whose presence would be conceivable outside and before the work
of *différance*, outside and before the process or system of
signification. The latter would only bring meaning to
light, translate it, transport it, communicate it, incarnate
it, express it, etc. Such a meaning—which in either case

is phenomenological meaning, and, in the last analysis, that which originally is given to consciousness in perceptive intuition—would not be, from the outset, in the position of a signifier, would not be inscribed in the relational and differential tissue which would make of it, from the outset, a referral, a trace, a gram, a spacing. It could be shown that metaphysics has always consisted in attempting to uproot the presence of meaning, in whatever guise, from *différance;* and every time that a region or layer of pure meaning or a pure signified is allegedly rigorously delineated or isolated this gesture is repeated. And how could semiotics, as such, *simply* dispense with any recourse to the identity of the signified? The relationship between meaning and sign, or between the signified and the signifier, then becomes one of *exteriority:* or better, as in Husserl, the latter becomes the exteriorization *(Äusserung)* or the expression *(Ausdruck)* of the former. Language is determined as expression—the expulsion of the intimacy of an inside—and we return to all the difficulties and presuppositions we were just speaking of concerning Saussure. I have attempted to indicate elsewhere the consequences that link all of phenomenology to this privilege of *expression,* to the exclusion of "indication" from the sphere of pure language (of the "logicity" of language), and to the privilege necessarily accorded to the voice, etc. This privilege was already at work in the *Logical Researches,* in the remarkable project of a "purely logical grammar" that is more important and more rigorous than all the projects of a "general reasoned grammar" of seventeenth- and eighteenth-century France, projects that certain modern linguists refer to, however.

Kristeva: If language is always "expression," and if its closure is thereby demonstrated, to what extent, and by means of what kind of practice, could this expressivity be surpassed? To what extent would nonexpressivity signify? Would not grammatology be a nonexpressive "semiology" based on logical-mathematical notation rather than on linguistic notation?

Derrida: I am tempted to respond in an apparently contradictory way. *On the one hand,* expressivism is never simply surpassable, because it is impossible to reduce the couple outside/inside as a simple structure of opposition. This couple is an effect of *différance,* as is the effect of language that impels language to represent itself as expressive re-presentation, a translation on the outside of what was constituted inside. The representation of language as "expression" is not an accidental prejudice, but rather a kind of structural lure, what Kant would have called a transcendental illusion. The latter is modified according to the language, the era, the culture. Doubtless Western metaphysics constitutes a powerful systematization of this illusion, but I believe that it would be an imprudent overstatement to assert that Western metaphysics alone does so. *On the other hand,* and inversely, I would say that if expressivism is not *simply and once and for all* surpassable, expressivity is in fact always already surpassed, whether one wishes it or not, whether one knows it or not. In the extent to which what is called "meaning" (to be "expressed") is already, and thoroughly, constituted by a tissue of differences, in the extent to which there is already a *text,* a network of textual referrals to *other* texts, a textual transformation in which each allegedly "simple term" is marked by the trace of another term, the presumed interiority of meaning is already worked upon by its own exteriority. It is always already carried outside itself. It already differs (from itself) before any act of expression. And only on this condition can it constitute a syntagm or text. Only on this condition can it "signify." From this point of view, perhaps, we would not have to ask to what extent nonexpressivity could signify. Only nonexpressivity can signify, because in all rigor there is no signification unless there is synthesis, syntagm, *différance,* and text. And the

notion of text, conceived with all its implications, is incompatible with the unequivocal notion of expression. Of
course, when one says that only the text signifies, one
already has transformed the values of signifying and
sign. For if one understands the sign in its most severe
classical closure, one would have to say the opposite:
signification is expression; the text, which expresses
nothing, is insignificant, etc. Grammatology, as the science of textuality, then would be a nonexpressive semiology only on the condition of transforming the concept of
sign and of uprooting it from its congenital expressivism.

The last part of your question is even more difficult. It
is clear that the reticence, that is, the resistance to
logical-mathematical notation has always been the signature of logocentrism and phonologism in the event to
which they have dominated metaphysics and the classical
semiological and linguistic projects. The critique of nonphonetic mathematical writing (for example, Leibniz's
"characteristic") in Rousseau, Hegel, etc., recurs in a
nonfortuitous manner in Saussure, for whom it coincides
with a stated preference for natural languages (see *Cours,*
p. 57). A grammatology that would break with this system of presuppositions, then, must in effect liberate the
mathematization of language, and must also declare that
"the practice of science in fact has never ceased to protest
the imperialism of the *Logos,* for example by calling
upon, from all time, and more and more, nonphonetic
writing."[5] Everything that has always linked *logos* to
phonē has been limited by mathematics, whose progress
is in absolute solidarity with the practice of a nonphonetic inscription. About these "grammatological" principles
and tasks there is no possible doubt, I believe. But the
extension of mathematical notation, and in general the
formalization of writing, must be very slow and very
prudent, at least if one wishes it to take over *effectively*
the domains from which it has been excluded so far. It
seems to me that critical work on "natural" languages by

means of "natural" languages, an entire internal transformation of classical notation, a systematic practice of
exchanges between "natural" languages and writing
should prepare and accompany such a formalization. An
infinite task, for it always will be impossible, and for
essential reasons, to reduce absolutely the natural languages and nonmathematical notation. We must also be
wary of the "naive" side of formalism and mathematism,
one of whose secondary functions in metaphysics, let us
not forget, has been to complete and confirm the
logocentric theology which they otherwise could contest.
Thus in Leibniz the project of a universal, mathematical,
and nonphonetic characteristic is inseparable from a
metaphysics of the simple, and hence from the existence
of divine understanding,[6] the divine *logos.*

The effective progress of mathematical notation thus
goes along with the deconstruction of metaphysics, with
the profound renewal of mathematics itself, and the concept of science for which mathematics has always been
the model.

Kristeva: The putting into question of the sign being a
putting into question of scientificity, to what extent is or
is not grammatology a "science"? Do you consider certain semiotic works close to the grammatological project,
and if so, which ones?

Derrida: Grammatology must deconstruct everything
that ties the concept and norms of scientificity to onto-
theology, logocentrism, phonologism. This is an immense and interminable work that must ceaselessly avoid
letting the transgression of the classical project of science
fall back into a prescientific empiricism. This supposes a
kind of *double register* in grammatological practice: it
must simultaneously go beyond metaphysical positivism
and scientism, and accentuate whatever in the effective
work of science contributes to freeing it of the metaphysical bonds that have borne on its definition and
its movement since its beginnings. Grammatology must

pursue and consolidate whatever, in scientific practice, has always already begun to exceed the logocentric closure. This is why there is no simple answer to the question of whether grammatology is a "science." In a word, I would say that it *inscribes* and *delimits* science; it must freely and rigorously make the norms of science function in its own writing; once again, it *marks* and at the same time *loosens* the limit which closes classical scientificity.

For the same reason, there is no *scientific* semiotic work that does not serve grammatology. And it will always be possible to turn against the metaphysical presuppositions of a semiotic discourse the grammatological motifs which science produces in semiotics. It is on the basis of the formalist and differential motif present in Saussure's *Cours* that the psychologism, phonologism and exclusion of writing that are no less present in it can be criticized. Similarly, in Hjelmslev's glossematics, if one drew all the consequences of the critique of Saussure's psychologism, the neutralization of expressive substances—and therefore of phonologism—the "structuralism," "immanentism," the critique of metaphysics, the thematics of play, etc., then one would be able to exclude an entire metaphysical conceptuality that is naively utilized (the couple expression/content in the tradition of the couple signifier/signified; the opposition form/substance applied to each of the two preceding terms; the "empirical principle," etc.).[7] One can say *a priori* that in every proposition or in every system of semiotic research—and you could cite the most current examples better than I—metaphysical presuppositions coexist with critical motifs. And this by the simple fact that up to a certain point they inhabit the same language. Doubtless, grammatology is less another science, a new discipline charged with a new content or new domain, than the vigilant practice of this textual division.

POSITIONS

Interview with
Jean-Louis Houdebine
and
Guy Scarpetta

Certain complements have been added to the transcript of this interview, which took place 17 June 1971:

1. Some notes proposed afterwards by Jacques Derrida. Their purpose is to specify certain points that improvisation had to skip over.

2. The editor's notes. They point out certain analyses in Derrida's texts that can clarify certain implications of the interview, spelling out the economy of a development, or, more frequently, demonstrating the delays and confusion that mark certain recent objections.

3. Fragments of an exchange of letters that followed the discussion.

First published in *Promesse* 30–31, Autumn and Winter 1971. The editor's notes have been reproduced.

Houdebine: To open this interview, perhaps we could take off, as from a point of insistence in the text unceasingly written and read here and there for several years now—perhaps we could take off from the "word" or "concept" of *différance* "which is ... literally neither a word nor a concept"; and therefore from the lecture delivered 27 January 1968, reprinted the same year in *Théorie d'ensemble:* [1] there you spoke of gathering into a "sheaf" the different directions that your research had taken up to then, and of the general system of its economy, even announcing, as concerns "the efficacity of the thematic of *différance*," the possibility of its *relève,* [2] since, in effect, it is to "lend itself, if not to its own replacement, at least to its linkage to a chain that, in all truth, it never will have governed."

Could you specify, at least under the rubric of an introduction to this interview, the actual state of your research, whose effectiveness immediately showed itself to have considerable bearing on the ideological field of our era, the state of development of the general economy again recently demarcated in three texts that are perhaps the symptoms of a new differentiation of the sheaf: your reading of Sollers's *Numbers,* in *"La dissémination,"* and then (but these two texts are contemporaries) *"La double séance"* and finally *"La mythologie blanche"*? [3]

Derrida: The motif of *différance,* when marked by a

silent *a*,[4] in effect plays neither the role of a "concept,"
nor simply of a "word." I have tried to demonstrate this.
This does not prevent it from producing conceptual effects
and verbal or nominal concretions. Which, moreover—
although this is not immediately noticeable—are simultaneously imprinted and fractured by the corner of this
"letter," by the incessant work of its strange "logic." The
"sheaf" which you recall is a historic and systematic
crossroads; and it is above all the structural impossibility
of limiting this network, of putting an edge on its weave,
of tracing a margin that would not be a new mark. Since
it cannot be elevated into a master-word or a master-
concept, since it blocks every relationship to theology,
différance finds itself enmeshed in the work that pulls it
through a chain of other "concepts," other "words," other
textual configurations. Perhaps later I will have occasion
to indicate why such other "words" or "concepts" later or
simultaneously imposed themselves; and why room had
to be left for their insistence (for example, *gram, reserve,
incision, trace, spacing, blank—sens blanc, sang blanc, sans
blanc, cent blancs, semblant*[5]*—supplement, pharmakon,
margin-mark-march*, etc.). By definition the list has no
taxonomical closure, and even less does it constitute a
lexicon. First, because these are not *atoms*, but rather
focal points of economic condensation, sites of passage
necessary for a very large number of marks, slightly more
effervescent crucibles.[6] Further, their effects do not simply turn back on themselves by means of an auto-
affection without opening. Rather they spread out in a
chain over the practical and theoretical entirety of a text,
and each time in a different way. Let me note in passing
that the word *"relève,"* in the sentence you cited, does
not have, by virtue of its context, the more technical
sense that I reserve for it in order to translate and interpret the Hegelian *Aufhebung*. If there were a definition of
différance, it would be precisely the limit, the interruption, the destruction of the Hegelian *relève wherever* it

operates.[7] What is at stake here is enormous. I emphasize the Hegelian *Aufhebung,* such as it is interpreted by a certain Hegelian discourse, for it goes without saying that the double meaning of *Aufhebung* could be written otherwise. Whence its proximity to all the operations conducted *against* Hegel's dialectical speculation.

What interested me then, that I am attempting to pursue along other lines now, was, at the same time as a "general economy," a kind of *general strategy of deconstruction.* The latter is to avoid both simply *neutralizing* the binary oppositions of metaphysics and simply *residing* within the closed field of these oppositions, thereby confirming it.

Therefore we must proceed using a double gesture, according to a unity that is both systematic and in and of itself divided, a double writing, that is, a writing that is in and of itself multiple, what I called, in *"La double séance,"* a *double science.*[8] On the one hand, we must traverse a phase of *overturning.* To do justice to this necessity is to recognize that in a classical philosophical opposition we are not dealing with the peaceful coexistence of a *vis-à-vis,* but rather with a violent hierarchy. One of the two terms governs the other (axiologically, logically, etc.), or has the upper hand. To deconstruct the opposition, first of all, is to overturn the hierarchy at a given moment. To overlook this phase of overturning is to forget the conflictual and subordinating structure of opposition. Therefore one might proceed too quickly to a *neutralization* that *in practice* would leave the previous field untouched, leaving one no hold on the previous opposition, thereby preventing any means of *intervening* in the field effectively. We know what always have been the *practical* (particularly *political*) effects of *immediately* jumping *beyond* oppositions, and of protests in the simple form of *neither* this *nor* that. When I say that this phase is necessary, the word *phase* is perhaps not the most rigorous one. It is not a question of a chronological

phase, a given moment, or a page that one day simply
will be turned, in order to go on to other things. The
necessity of this phase is structural; it is the necessity of
an interminable analysis: the hierarchy of dual oppositions always reestablishes itself. Unlike those authors
whose death does not await their demise, the time for
overturning is never a dead letter.

That being said—and on the other hand—to remain in
this phase is still to operate on the terrain of and from
within the deconstructed system. By means of this double, and precisely stratified, dislodged and dislodging,
writing, we must also mark the interval between inver-
sion, which brings low what was high, and the irruptive
emergence of a new "concept," a concept that can no
longer be, and never could be, included in the previous
regime. If this interval, this biface or biphase, can be inscribed only in a bifurcated writing (and this holds first
of all for a new concept of writing, that *simultaneously*
provokes the overturning of the hierarchy speech/writing,
and the entire system attached to it, *and* releases the dis-
sonance of a writing within speech, thereby disorganizing the entire inherited order and invading the entire
field), then it can only be marked in what I would call a
grouped textual field: in the last analysis it is impossible
to *point* it out, for a unilinear text, or a punctual *position*,[9]
an operation signed by a single author, are all by definition incapable of practicing this interval.

Henceforth, in order better to mark this interval (*La dissémination*, the text that bears this title, since you have
asked me about it, is a systematic and playful exploration
of the interval—"*écart*," *carré, carrure, carte, charte,
quatre*,[10] etc.) it has been necessary to analyze, to set to
work, *within* the text of the history of philosophy, as well
as *within* the so-called literary text (for example, Mallarmé), certain marks, shall we say (I mentioned certain
ones just now, there are many others), that *by analogy* (I

underline) I have called undecidables, that is, unities of simulacrum, "false" verbal properties (nominal or semantic) that can no longer be included within philosophical (binary) opposition, but which, however, inhabit philosophical opposition, resisting and disorganizing it, *without ever* constituting a third term, without ever leaving room for a solution in the form of speculative dialectics (the *pharmakon* is neither remedy nor poison, neither good nor evil, neither the inside nor the outside, neither speech nor writing; the *supplement* is neither a plus nor a minus, neither an outside nor the complement of an inside, neither accident nor essence, etc.; the *hymen* is neither confusion nor distinction, neither identity nor difference, neither consummation nor virginity, neither the veil nor unveiling, neither the inside nor the outside, etc.; the *gram* is neither a signifier nor a signified, neither a sign nor a thing, neither a presence nor an absence, neither a position nor a negation, etc.; *spacing* is neither space nor time; the *incision* is neither the incised integrity of a beginning, or of a simple cutting into, nor simple secondarity. Neither/nor, that is, *simultaneously* either *or*; the mark is also the *marginal* limit, the *march*, etc.).[11] In fact, I attempt to bring the critical operation to bear against the unceasing reappropriation of this work of the simulacrum by a dialectics of the Hegelian type (which even idealizes and "semantizes" the value of *work*), for Hegelian idealism consists precisely of a *relève* of the binary oppositions of classical idealism, a resolution of contradiction into a third term that comes in order to *aufheben*, to deny while raising up, while idealizing, while sublimating into an anamnesic interiority *(Errinnerung)*, while *interning* difference in a self-presence.[12]

Since it is still a question of elucidating the relationship to Hegel—a difficult labor, which for the most part remains before us, and which in a certain way is

interminable, at least if one wishes to execute it rigorously and minutely—I have attempted to distinguish
différance (whose *a* marks, among other things, its productive and conflictual characteristics) from Hegelian difference, and have done so precisely at the point at
which Hegel, in the greater *Logic,* determines difference
as contradiction[13] only in order to resolve it, to interi-
orize it, to lift it up (according to the syllogistic process of
speculative dialectics) into the self-presence of an onto-
theological or onto-teleological synthesis. *Différance* (at a
point of almost absolute proximity to Hegel, as I have
emphasized, I think, in the lecture and elsewhere:[14] everything, what is most decisive, is played out, here, in
what Husserl called "subtle nuances," or Marx "microl-
ogy") must sign the point at which one breaks with the
system of the *Aufhebung* and with speculative dialectics.
Since this conflictuality of *différance*[15]—which can be
called contradiction only if one demarcates it by means of
a long work on Hegel's concept of contradiction—can
never be totally resolved, it marks its effects in what I call
the text in general, in a text which is not reduced to a
book or a library, and which can never be governed by a
referent in the classical sense, that is, by a thing or by a
transcendental signified that would regulate its movement. You can well see that it is not because I wish to
appease or reconcile that I prefer to employ the mark
"différance" rather than refer to the system of difference-
and-contradiction.

Then, in effect—I am still following your question—the
motif, or if you prefer, the concept, the operator of generality named *dissemination* inserted itself into the open
chain of *différance,* "supplement," "*pharmakon*,"
"hymen," etc. This happened most notably, as you
know, by means of a kind of cooperative reading of Sollers's *Nombres,* in the text published in *Critique* that you
mentioned. In the last analysis *dissemination* means
nothing, and cannot be reassembled into a definition. I

will not attempt to do so here, and I prefer to refer to the work of the texts. If dissemination, seminal *différance*, cannot be summarized into an exact conceptual tenor, it is because the force and form of its disruption *explode* the semantic horizon. The attention brought to bear on polysemia or polythematism doubtless represents progress in relationship to the linearity of the monothematic writing or reading that is always anxious to anchor itself to the tutelary meaning, the *principal* signified of a text, that is, its major referent. Nevertheless, polysemia, as such, is organized within the implicit horizon of a unitary resumption of meaning, that is, within the horizon of a dialectics—Richard speaks of a dialectics in his thematic reading of Mallarmé, Ricoeur too, in his essay on Freud (and Ricoeur's hermeneutics, his theory of polysemia, has much in common with thematic criticism, as Richard acknowledges)—a teleological and totalizing dialectics that at a given moment, however far off, must permit the reassemblage of the totality of a text into the truth of its meaning, constituting the text as *expression*, as *illustration*, and annulling the open and productive displacement of the textual chain. Dissemination, on the contrary, although producing a nonfinite number of semantic effects, can be led back neither to a present of simple origin ("*La dissémination*," "*La double séance*," and "*La mythologie blanche*" are practical re-presentations of all the false departures, beginnings, first lines, titles, epigraphs, fictive pretexts, etc.: decapitations) nor to an eschatological presence. It marks an irreducible and *generative* multiplicity. The supplement and the turbulence of a certain lack fracture the limit of the text, forbidding an exhaustive and closed formalization of it, or at least a saturating taxonomy of its themes, its signified, its meaning.

Here, of course, we are *playing* on the fortuitous resemblance, the purely simulated common parentage of *seme* and *semen*. There is no communication of meaning

between them. And yet, by means of this floating, purely
exterior collusion, accident produces a kind of semantic
mirage: the deviance of meaning, its reflection-effect in
writing, sets something off.

I have attempted not to formalize this motivic regime
of the surplus (and the) lack in the neutrality of a critical
discourse (I have said why an exhaustive formalization in
the classical sense is impossible;[16] "*La double séance*" is a
deconstructive "critique" of the notion of "criticism"),
but rather to rewrite it, to inscribe and *relaunch* its
schemes. In "*La dissémination*" and "*La double séance*"
(these two texts are inseparable) it is a question of re-
marking a nerve, a fold, an angle that interrupts totaliza-
tion: in a certain place, a place of well-determined form,
no series of semantic valences can any longer be closed or
reassembled. Not that it opens onto an inexhaustible
wealth of meaning or the transcendence of a semantic excess. By means of this angle, this fold, this doubled fold
of an undecidable, a mark marks both the marked and
the mark, the re-marked site of the mark. The writing
which, at this moment, re-marks itself (something completely other than a representation of itself) can no longer
be counted on the list of themes (it is not a theme, and
can in no case become one); it must be subtracted from
(hollow) and added to (relief) the list. The hollow is the
relief, but the lack and the surplus can never be stabilized
in the plenitude of a form or an equation, in the station-
ary correspondence of a symmetry or a homology. Here, I
cannot repeat what I have attempted in these two texts,
the work on the fold, the blank, the hymen, the margin,
the chandelier, the column, the angle, the square, the air,
the supernumber, etc. This work always has this
theoretical result among others: a criticism concerned
only with content (that is, a thematic criticism, be it in
philosophical, sociological, or psychoanalytic style, that
takes the theme—manifest or hidden, full or empty—as

the substance of the text, as its object or as its *illustrated truth*) can no more measure itself against *certain* texts (or rather the structure of certain textual *scenes*) than can a purely formalist criticism which would be interested only in the code, the pure play of signifiers, the technical manipulation of a text-object, thereby overlooking the genetic effects or the ("historical," if you will) inscription of the text read *and* of the new text this criticism itself writes. These two insufficiencies are rigorously complementary. They cannot be defined without a deconstruction of classical rhetoric and its implicit philosophy: I began this deconstruction in *"La double séance"* and have attempted to systematize it in *"La mythologie blanche."* The critique of formalist structuralism was undertaken from the first texts of *Writing and Difference*.

Scarpetta: In order further to contribute to the historical situation of this interview, we might equally invoke the meeting which took place at Cluny in April 1970. Although absent, you were constantly present (cited or questioned in sometimes quite contradictory interventions) at this colloquium, whose object was the relationship between "Literature and Ideologies."

Houdebine: Following the axis of this question opened by Scarpetta, and since this point was raised at Cluny, I would like to return to the problem of the confrontation of your reflections with the philosophy of Heidegger. In the text already cited, *"La différance,"* you speak of the "uncircumventable Heideggerean meditation." What makes this meditation, as it unfolds at the heart of an "era," which is our own, seem to you "uncircumventable"? And since, on the other hand, you call it "uncircumventable" only in order to traverse it, could you specify some of the motifs that keep you from remaining in it?

Derrida: You are right to refer to the colloquium, whose acts[17] I have just read. It seems to me a very important

event, both theoretically and politically. As for the relationships between "literature" and "ideology," there is
a considerable elucidation to be made and numerous
interventions which, I believe, will help move things
along.

Your questions are multiple and difficult. Where to
begin? Come back to what concerns me? Do you think it
is still necessary?

Houdebine: Perhaps it would permit us to clear up certain misunderstandings and, as you just said, to help
"move things along" a little bit more.

Derrida: All right then. Naturally I did not wish to
bring up here whatever may have concerned me in the
course of a debate, which happily was not limited to this,
and which, as you know, I was very sorry not to be able
to participate in directly. If I answer your question, it is
above all in order to distinguish between the kinds of
interrogations or objections that were addressed to me.
Certain ones, like Christine Glucksmann's, are obviously
destined, without an embarrassed aggressiveness, to
make reading and discussion possible. I will answer
them in a moment, as I will do moreover whenever an
exchange is presented in these conditions, and when I
am in a position to bring something to it. As concerns
other interventions that seem to me backwards or re-
gressive, I will only recall certain points, moreover
elementary ones.

Even if said in passing, I learned, having read it at least
twice, that my "thought" (I am quoting, naturally) was in
"full evolution." Is this not cause for rejoicing?[18] It is true
that these statements are made from a vantage at which
one must fully well know at what term or at what turn
this "evolution" is to be expected, and against what
eschatology to measure it. I would benefit greatly from
such encouragement—well-meaning in one case, senten-
tious in the other—if the value "evolution" had not

always seemed suspect to me (is it Marxist, tell me?), and if, above all, I had not always been wary of "thought." No, it is a question of textual displacements whose course, form, and necessity have nothing to do with the "evolution" of "thought" or the teleology of a discourse. It is now quite some time, permit me to recall, since I risked the following sentence, that is, that I *wrote* it, for the silent work of italics and quotation marks should not be subtracted from it, as happens too often (for instead of investigating only the content of thoughts, it is also necessary to analyze the way in which texts are *made*): *"In a certain way, 'thought' means nothing."* [19] "Thought" (quotation marks: the words "thought" and what is called "thought") means nothing: it is the substantified void of a highly derivative ideality, the effect of a *différance* of forces, the illusory autonomy of a discourse or a consciousness whose hypostasis is to be deconstructed, whose "causality" is to be analyzed, etc. First. Secondly, the sentence can be read thus: if there is thought—and there is, and it is just as suspect, for analogous critical reasons, to contest the authority of all "thought"—then whatever will continue to be called thought, and which, for example, will designate the deconstruction of logocentrism, means nothing, for in the last analysis it no longer derives from "meaning." Wherever it operates, *"thought" means nothing.*

I come now to Christine Glucksmann's nuanced reservations: "history conceived too linearly as the history of meaning," "a conception of a latent history . . . that seems to underestimate, if not to erase, the struggle between materialism and idealism . . ." (p. 240). Must I recall that from the first texts I published, I have attempted to systematize a deconstructive critique precisely against the authority of meaning, as the *transcendental signified* or as *telos,* in other words history determined in the last analysis as the history of meaning, history in its

logocentric, metaphysical, idealist (I will come back to
these words in a moment) representation, even up to the
complex marks it has left in Heidegger's discourse. I do
not wish to enlarge upon this, nor to give any references,
for what I have just spelled out is legible on every page. I
can be reproached for being insistent, even monotonous,
but it is difficult for me to see how a concept of history as
the "history of meaning" can be attributed to me.
Truthfully, at the root of the misunderstanding might be
the following: I am constituted as the proprietor of what I
analyze, to wit, a metaphysical concept of history as
ideal, teleological history, etc. As this concept is much
more generally extended than is usually believed, and
certainly far beyond the philosophies labeled "idealist," I
am very wary of the concept of history; and the marks of
this wariness, which doubtless we will have occasion to
come back to, may have provoked the misunderstandings
of a first reading.

As for linearism, you know very well that it is not my
strong point.[20] I have always, and very precisely, associated it with logocentrism, phonocentrism, seman-
tism, and idealism. Not only have I never believed in the
absolute autonomy[21] of a history as the history of philosophy, in a conventionally Hegelian sense, but I have also
regularly tried to put philosophy back on stage, on a
stage that it does not govern, and that the classical histo-
rians of philosophy, in the university and elsewhere,
have sometimes judged a little difficult. This is why I was
not accustomed to the suspicions that Christine
Glucksmann formulated.

" . . . underestimate, if not to erase, the struggle between materialism and idealism"? No, not at all, it interests me a great deal, on the contrary, and it has been, for
a long time now, of an importance that cannot be over-
estimated. I am even interested in certain forms of so-
called mechanical materialism, from which there is still

much to be got. It is probable that I have had nothing very original or specifically new to propose on this subject. In that case, I am not very loquacious, which is doubtless what is regretted. Don't you see, what has seemed necessary and urgent to me, in the historical situation which is our own, is a general determination of the conditions for the emergence and the limits of philosophy, of metaphysics, of everything that carries it on and that it carries on. In *Of Grammatology* I simultaneously proposed everything that can be reassembled under the rubric of *logocentrism*—and I cannot pursue this any further here—along with the project of *deconstruction*. Here, there is a powerful historical and systematic unity that must be determined first if one is not to take dross for gold every time that an emergence, rupture, break, mutation, etc. is allegedly delineated.[22] Logocentrism is *also,* fundamentally, an idealism. It is the matrix of idealism. Idealism is its most direct representation, the most constantly dominant force. And the dismantling of logocentrism is simultaneously—*a fortiori*—a deconstitution of idealism or spiritualism in all their variants. Really, it is not a question of "erasing" the "struggle" against idealism. Now of course, logocentrism is a wider concept than idealism, for which it serves as a kind of overflowing foundation. And a wider concept than phonocentrism, too. It constitutes a system of predicates, certain of which can always be found in the philosophies that *call themselves* nonidealist, that is, antiidealist. The handling of the concept of logocentrism, therefore, is delicate and sometimes troubling.

Shall we say a word now about the other category of objections raised at the Cluny colloquium? Since I have already explained myself on this topic, and since I find the expression rather comical, I will not come back to the "rejection of history" attributed to me (p. 230). Nor can I go through, line by line, all the propositions whose confusion, I must say, rather disconcerted me. This, for example: "The Derridean grammatic is 'modeled,' in its major lines, on Heideggerean metaphysics, which it attempts to 'deconstruct' by substituting the anteriority of a trace for the 'presence of the logos'; it constitutes itself as an onto-theology based on the trace as 'ground,' 'foundation' or 'origin'" (p. 225). How does one model oneself after what one deconstructs? Can one speak so simply of Heideggerean *metaphysics*? But above all (because these first two eventualities are not absurd in themselves, even if they are so here) have I not indefatigably repeated—and I would dare say demonstrated—that the trace is neither a ground, nor a foundation, nor an origin, and that in no case can it provide for a manifest or disguised onto-theology? It is true that this confusion, which consists in turning against my texts criticisms one forgets one has found in them first and borrowed from them—this confusion already had been feigned, at least, by readers who were a bit better informed, if not better armed.

Nor have I ever said that "Saussure's project," in its principle or in its entirety, was "logocentrist" or "phonocentrist."

The work of my reading does not take this form. (When I try to decipher a text I do not constantly ask myself if I will finish by answering *yes* or *no*, as happens in France at determined periods of history, and generally on Sunday.) Saussure's text, like any other, is not homogeneous. Yes, I did analyze a "logocentrist" and "phonocentrist" layer of it (which had not been demarcated, and whose bearing is considerable), but I did so in order to show immediately that it was in contradiction to Saussure's scientific project, such as it may be read and such as I took it into account. I cannot demonstrate this again here.[23]

I have never, directly or indirectly, as is alleged for reasons that remain to be analyzed, identified writing with myth. Here, I understand the concept of writing as I have attempted to determine it. Inversely, I sometimes have been interested in the gesture by means of which philosophy excluded writing from its field, or from the field of scientific rationality, in order to keep it in an exterior that *sometimes* took the form of *myth.* This is the operation that I investigated, particularly in *"La pharmacie de Platon,"* which demanded new ways, and could proceed neither along the lines of *mythology,* of course, nor the *philosophical* concept of science.[24] In particular, the issue is to deconstruct practically the *philosophical* opposition between philosophy and myth, between *logos* and *mythos.* Practically, I insist, this can only be done textually, along the lines of an *other* writing, with all the implied risks. And I fear that these risks will grow greater still.

Abasement, the abasement of writing: evidently it is not a question—which would be contradictory to the entire context—of raising up writing from what I, myself, considered to be its abasement. Abasement is precisely the *representation* of writing, of its situation *in* the philosophical hierarchy (high/low). Here, too, what I denounce is attributed to me, as if one were in less of a hurry to criticize or to discuss me, than first to put oneself in my place in order to do so. It is a question, therefore, as concerns this value of abasement or fall, of what philosophy (and everything that is part of its system) thought it was doing, intended to do, by operating from the vantage of life present to itself in its logos, of ontological or original plenitude: which is precisely what the deconstructing operation has defined itself against. And the notion of "fall," which is thoroughly complementary to the notion of "origin," was a constant target, in *Of Grammatology* and elsewhere. Consequently I have never incorporated the theme of a prelapsarian writing that would have fallen, through I know not what original sin, into the debased and degraded field of history. On the contrary.

Since this is too evident for anyone who wishes to begin to read, I will not insist, and go on to the relationship with Heidegger.

I do maintain, as you recalled in your question, that Heidegger's text is extremely important to me, and that it constitutes a novel, irreversible advance all of whose critical resources we are far from having exploited.

That being said—and apart from the fact that for all kinds of reasons, and, I believe, in numerous ways, what I write does not, shall we say, *resemble* a text of Heideggerean filiation (I cannot analyze this in detail here)—I have marked quite explicitly, in *all* the essays I have published, as can be verified, a *departure* from the Heideggerean problematic. This departure is related particularly to the concepts of *origin* and *fall* of which we were just speaking. And, among other places, I have analyzed it as concerns time, "the transcendental horizon of the question of Being," in *Being and Time,* that is, at a strategically decisive point.[25] This departure also, and correlatively, intervenes as concerns the value *proper* (propriety, propriate, appropriation, the entire family of *Eigentlichkeit, Eigen, Ereignis*) which is perhaps the most continuous and most difficult thread of Heidegger's thought. (I will take this occasion to specify, in passing, that I have also explicitly criticized this value of propriety and of original authenticity, and that I even, if it can be put thus, started there. This fanatacism or monotony might be startling, but I cannot seriously be made to say the opposite: "Grammatology, the general science of the 'archi-trace,' presents itself as an explicating thought of the myth of origins. It is a search not for 'historical origins,' but for the *original,* the true, the *authentic etymon* always already present which obscures it." [E. Roudinesco, p. 223.] Here, misunderstanding takes on grandiose proportions.) Wherever the values of propriety, of a proper meaning, of proximity to the self, of etymology, etc. imposed themselves in relation to the body, consciousness, language, writing, etc., I have attempted to analyze the metaphysical desire and presuppositions that were at work. This can already be ascertained in *"La parole soufflée"* (1965; in *Writing and Difference*), but also everywhere else. *"La mythologie blanche"* systematizes the critique of etymologism in philosophy and rhetoric.[26] Naturally, to come back to Heidegger, doubtless the most decisive and most difficult point is that of meaning, the present and presence. In *"Ousia* and *Grammē"*[27] I proposed a very schematic problematic, or rather a kind of grid, for reading Heidegger's texts from this point of view. This entails an immense labor, and things will never be simple. Since in the course of an interview like this one I can only formulate, shall we say, a traveler's impressions, I sometimes have the feeling that the Heideggerean problematic is the most "profound" and "powerful" defense of what I attempt to put into question under the rubric of the *thought of presence.*

Happily, we are far from the analogizing confusion which keeps itself busy: (1) by reducing, using no other procedure, grammatological deconstruction to a prefabricated Heideggereanism, which is obviously *completely misunderstood;* (2) by alleging that there is *nothing more* in Heidegger than the German ideology of the period between the two wars; (3) by insinuating that Heidegger had reservations about psychoanalysis simply because it is "Jewish" (which would lead one to believe, by atmospheric contagion—an element of analysis like any other—that anyone who dallies with an attentive reading of Heidegger remains suspect on this score. The insistence with which this is maintained—see *L'Humanité* of 12 September 1969, and the double protest that followed, published one week later in *L'Humanité* of 19 September 1969, and reprinted in *Tel Quel* no. 39, and developed in all its implications in *Tel Quel* no. 40[28]—will finally make me aware of an antisemitism that is still all too visceral.) To conclude, there is here a self-perpetuating deviance, a kind of spellbound projection, which is taking a more and more defamatory turn. I have been listening to this kind of discourse for some time now, with a more or less free-floating attention. And have kept a certain silence. Which is not to be abused.

Let us leave, if you will, these doctors of scientific genealogy or ideological filiation. Students will learn from them that for Heidegger dialectics has a Jewish essence (p. 189), or that Plato is the inheritor of the Stoics and the Epicureans ("The science of letters, simple elements, or *grammatikē technē* founded by the Stoics and the Epicureans, taken over by Plato, theorized by Aristotle." p. 221).[29] You see, what seems lacking to me in the *"problematic of the narrative"* is the ability to reflect precisely that which makes its very theses unnarratable. Could Borges have authored such a singular narrative? Alas . . .

Scarpetta: Perhaps we could come back to what you have said about history. I am thinking of the text in *Of Grammatology* in which you say: "The word 'history' doubtless has always been associated with the linear consecution of presence." Can you conceive of the possibility of a concept of history that would escape this linear scheme? Can you see the possibility of what Sollers calls, for example, "monumental history," that is, history conceived no longer as a linear scheme, but as a stratified, differentiated, contradictory practical series, that is, neither a monistic nor a historicist history?

Derrida: Of course. What we must be wary of, I repeat, is the *metaphysical* concept of history. This is the concept of history as the history of meaning, as we were just saying a moment ago: the history of meaning developing itself, producing itself, fulfilling itself. And doing so linearly, as you recall: in a straight or circular line. This is why, moreover, the "closure of metaphysics" cannot

have the form of a *line,* that is, the form in which philosophy recognizes it, in which philosophy recognizes itself.
The closure of metaphysics, above all, is not a circle surrounding a homogeneous field, a field homogeneous
with itself on its inside, whose outside then would be
homogeneous also. The limit has the form of always different faults, of fissures whose mark or scar is borne by
all the texts of philosophy.

The metaphysical character of the concept of history is
not only linked to linearity, but to an entire *system* of
implications (teleology, eschatology, elevating and interiorizing accumulation of meaning, a certain type of tradi-
tionality, a certain concept of continuity, of truth, etc.).
Therefore it is not an accidental predicate which could be
removed by a kind of local ablation, without a general
displacement of the organization, without setting the entire system to work. It has happened that I have spoken
very quickly of a "metaphysical concept." But I have
never believed that there were *metaphysical* concepts *in
and of themselves.* No concept is by itself,[30] and consequently in and of itself, metaphysical, outside all the
textual work in which it is inscribed. This explains why,
although I have formulated many reservations about the
"metaphysical" concept of history, I very *often* use the
word "history" in order to reinscribe its force[31] and
in order to produce another concept or conceptual chain
of "history": in effect a "monumental, stratified, contradictory" history; a history that also implies a new
logic of *repetition* and the *trace,* for it is difficult to see
how there could be history without it.

Nevertheless we must recognize that the concept of
history, by the force of the system of predicates I just
mentioned, can always be reappropriated by
metaphysics. For example: we must first distinguish
between history in general and the general concept of
history. Althusser's entire, and necessary, critique of the

"Hegelian" concept of history and of the notion of an expressive totality, etc., aims at showing that there is not one single history, a general history, but rather histories *different* in their type, rhythm, mode of inscription—intervallic, differentiated histories. I have always subscribed to this, as to the concept of history that Sollers calls "monumental."[32]

To ask another kind of question: on the basis of what minimal semantic kernel will these heterogeneous, irreducible histories still be named "histories"? How can the minimum that they must have in common be determined if the common noun history is to be conferred in a way that is not purely conventional or purely confused? It is here that the question of the system of essential predicates that I mentioned above is reintroduced. Socrates asks what science is. He is answered: there is this science, and then that one, and yet again that one. Socrates insists on having an impoverished answer which, cutting short empirical enumeration, would tell him about the scientificity of science, and why all these different sciences are called *science*. But in asking about the historicity of history, about what permits us to call "histories" these histories irreducible to the reality of a general history, the issue is precisely not to return to a question of the Socratic type. The issue is rather to show that the risk of metaphysical reappropriation is ineluctable, that it happens very fast, as soon as the question of the concept and of meaning, or of the essentiality that necessarily regulates the risk, is asked. As soon as the question of the historicity of history is asked—and how can it be avoided if one is manipulating a plural or heterogeneous concept of history?—one is impelled to respond with a definition of essence, of quiddity, to reconstitute a system of essential predicates, and one is also led to refurbish the semantic grounds of the philosophical tradition. A philosophical tradition that always, finally, amounts to an inclusion of historicity on an ontological ground, precisely. Henceforth, we must not only ask what is the "essence" of history, the historicity of history, but what is the "history" of "essence" in general? And if one wishes to mark a break between some "new concept of history" and the question of the essence of history (as with the concept that the essence regulates), the question of the history of essence and the history of the concept, finally the history of the meaning of Being, you have a measure of the work which remains to be done.

That being said, the concept of history, no more than any other, cannot be subject to a simple and instantaneous mutation, the striking of a name from the vocabulary. We must elaborate a strategy of the textual work which at every instant borrows an old word from philosophy in order immediately to demarcate it. This is what I was alluding to just now in speaking of a double gesture or double stratification. We must first *overturn* the traditional concept of history, but at the same time mark the *interval*, take care that by virtue of the overturning, and by the simple fact of conceptualization, that the interval not be *reappropriated*. Certainly a new conceptualization is to be produced, but it must take into account the fact that conceptualization itself, and by itself alone, can reintroduce what one wants to "criticize." This is why this work cannot be purely "theoretical" or "conceptual" or "discursive," I mean cannot be the work of a discourse entirely regulated by essence, meaning, truth, consciousness, ideality, etc. What I call *text* is also that which "practically" inscribes and overflows the limits of such a discourse. *There is* such a general text everywhere that (that is, everywhere) this discourse and its order (essence, sense, truth, meaning, consciousness, ideality, etc.) are *overflowed*, that is, everywhere that their authority is put back into the position of a *mark* in a chain that this authority intrinsically and illusorily believes it wishes to, and does in fact, govern. This general text is not limited, of course, as will (or would) be quickly understood, to writings on the page. The writing of this text, moreover, has the exterior limit only of a certain *re-mark*. Writing on the page, and then "literature," are determined types of this re-mark. They must be investigated in their specificity, and in a new way, if you will, in the specificity of their "history," and in their articulation with the other "historical" fields of the text in general.

This is why, briefly, I so often use the word "history," but so often too with the quotation marks and precautions that may have led to the attribution to me of (I am going to abuse this expression, which will lead me to prefer another: "good style") a "rejection of history."

Houdebine: These initial elaborations immediately place us on the different axes of the extension of your work: they also put us in a position to specify the historical, theoretical site from which we are led to emit our own questions, it being well understood that your work itself shakes the very site of our questioning.

Let us very briefly determine this site as that of dialectical materialism, of dialectical materialist logic, whose general economy is articulated on the basis of the conceptual series "matter (that is, an irreducible heterogeneity in relation to a subject-meaning)/contradiction/struggle of the contraries, unity-inseparability-convertibility of the contraries in the process of their transformation, etc."—this conceptual series to whose rereading Althusser has contributed so much—which is necessarily caught in an economy whose double register appears fundamentally in the *dual unity* recently marked by Sollers *(Tel Quel,* 43, *"Lénine et le materialisme philosophique): historical materialism/dialectical materialism.

The first sketch of a question: what relationship do you think is to be established between this economy of a dialectical materialist logic and the economy that you have based on a problematic of *writing*?

Let us try to delimit a first, and still quite vast, field of the question, since doubtless we will have occasion to come back to it over and over in the course of this interview (several problems are indicated in this question already, and the itinerary that we will follow will probably be a kind of constellation, to be mapped out by overlapping, by going over the questions and the answers): if it clearly appears—and everything you have just said confirms it—that a certain number of intersecting points or at least strategic convergences can be determined between these two types of economy, most notably on the basis of your deconstruction of the problematic of the sign as deriving from a fundamental logocentrism, from a philosophy of consciousness or of the originary subject—perhaps it would be time today to ask about the status of these points of intersection and/or strategic convergences.

And for example, it seems to us that the itinerary of a deconstruction of logocentric discourse inevitably encounters the materialist text, which has long been the historical text repressed-suppressed by logocentric discourse (idealism, metaphysics, religion) taken as the discourse of a ruling ideology in its different historical forms. Do you agree with us about the necessity of marking out this encounter? And could you tell us why this necessity has been marked in your work, up to now, either in a marginal fashion (I am thinking most notably of several notes in "*La double séance*" which bear witness, moreover, to the necessity you felt at that time of strategically—and even politically—regulating the implications of your discourse), or in a lacunary fashion, as in the passage of "*La différance*" where you speak of putting into question "the self-assured certitude of consciousness" and refer to Nietzsche and Freud, leaving in suspense (but this suspense itself is perfectly legible) any reference to Marx, and along with Marx to the text of dialectical materialism? But it is true that in Marx, as in Engels and Lenin, the putting into question of the self-certainty of consciousness is not "based on the motif of *différance*," and that another general economy is at stake here (has been at stake for a long time), according to the conceptual series briefly enunciated just now, and to which we would have to add the Marxist concept of "ideology."

Derrida: Naturally, I cannot answer these questions in a word. Where to begin? In effect, there is what you call this "encounter," which has seemed absolutely necessary to me for a long time. You can imagine that I have not been completely unconscious of it. That being said, I persist in believing that there is no theoretical or political benefit to be derived from precipitating contacts or articulations, as long as their conditions have not been rigorously elucidated. Eventually such precipitation will have the effect only of dogmatism, confusion, or opportunism. To impose this prudence upon oneself is to take seriously the difficulty, and also the heterogeneity, of the Marxist text, the decisive importance of its historical stakes.

Where to begin then? If one wished to schematize—but truly this is only a schema—what I have attempted can *also* be inscribed under the rubric of the "critique of idealism." Therefore it goes without saying that to the extent that dialectical materialism also operates this critique, it in no way incurs my reticence, nor have I ever formulated any on this subject.

Do me the credit of believing that the "lacunae" to which you alluded are explicitly calculated to mark the sites of a theoretical elaboration which remains, *for me*, at least, *still to come.* And they are indeed lacunae, not objections; they have a specific and deliberate status, I even dare say a certain efficacity. When I say *for me*, I under-

stand this: the conjunction between the work I
attempt—a limited work, but with its own field and
framework, a work possible only in a historical, political,
theoretical, etc., situation that is highly determined—and
the entire text and conceptuality of Marxism cannot be
immediately given. To believe so would be to erase the
specificity of these fields and to limit their *effective*
transformation. Now in both cases, shall we say, to proceed quickly, in question are "fields" that inscribe the
possibility and opening of their practical transformation.
And when I say *"still to come,"* I am still, and above all,
thinking of the relationship of Marx to Hegel, and of the
question we were speaking of just now (dialectics, difference, contradiction, etc.). Despite the immense work
which already has been done in this domain, a decisive
elaboration has not yet been accomplished, and for historical reasons which can be analyzed, precisely, only
during the elaboration of this work.

In what I have begun to propose, I attempt to take into
account certain recent acquisitions or determined in-
completions in the orders of philosophy, semiology,
linguistics, psychoanalysis, etc. . . . Now, we cannot consider Marx's, Engels's or Lenin's texts as completely
finished elaborations that are simply to be "applied" to
the current situation. In saying this, I am not advocating
anything contrary to "Marxism," I am convinced of it.
These texts are not to be read according to a hermenueti-
cal or exegetical method which would seek out a finished
signified beneath a textual surface. Reading is transformational. I believe that this would be confirmed by certain of Althusser's propositions. But this transformation
cannot be executed however one wishes. It requires pro-
tocols of reading. Why not say it bluntly: I have not yet
found any that satisfy me.

No more than I have dealt with Saussure's text, or
Freud's, or any other, as homogeneous volumes (the

motif of homogeneity, the theological motif *par excellence*, is decidedly the one to be destroyed), I do not find
the texts of Marx, Engels, or Lenin homogeneous cri-
tiques. In their relationship to Hegel, for example. And
the manner in which they themselves reflected and formulated the differentiated or contradictory structure of
their relationship to Hegel has not seemed to me, cor-
rectly or incorrectly, sufficient. Thus I will have to
analyze what I consider a heterogeneity, conceptualizing
both its necessity and the rules for deciphering it; and do
so by taking into account the decisive progress simultaneously accomplished by Althusser and those following
him. All this poses many questions, and today I could tell
you nothing not already legible in the lacunae or notes to
which you alluded, at least for anyone who wishes to
pursue their consequences. Above all they refer to the
general economy whose traits I attempted to outline
based on a reading of Bataille.[33] It follows that if, and in
the extent to which, *matter* in this general economy designates, as you said, radical alterity (I will specify: in relation to philosophical oppositions), then what I write
can be considered "materialist."

As you may imagine, things are not so simple. It is not
always in *the* materialist text (is there such a thing, *the*
materialist text?) nor in *every* materialist text that the concept of matter has been defined as absolute exterior or
radical heterogeneity. I am not even sure that there can
be a "concept" of an absolute exterior. If I have not very
often used the word "matter," it is not, as you know,
because of some idealist or spiritualist kind of reserva-
tion. It is that in the logic of the phase of overturning this
concept has been too often reinvested with "logocentric"
values, values associated with those of thing, reality,
presence in general, sensible presence, for example, sub-
stantial plenitude, content, referent, etc. Realism or
sensualism—"empiricism"—are modifications of

logocentrism. (I have often insisted on the fact that "writing" or the "text" are not reducible *either* to the sensible or visible presence of the graphic or the "literal.") In short, the signifier "matter" appears to me problematical only at the moment when its reinscription cannot avoid making of it a new fundamental principle which, by means of theoretical regression, would be reconstituted into a "transcendental signified." It is not only idealism in the narrow sense that falls back upon the transcendental signified. It can always come to reassure a metaphysical materialism. It then becomes an ultimate referent, according to the classical logic implied by the value of referent, or it becomes an "objective reality" absolutely "anterior" to any work of the mark, the semantic content of a form of presence which guarantees the movement of the text in general from the outside. (I am not sure that Lenin's analysis, for example, does not always give in to this operation; and if it does so strategically, we must first reelaborate—in a transformational writing—the rules of this strategy. Then there would be no reservations to be made.) This is why I will not say that the concept of matter is in and of itself either metaphysical or nonmetaphysical. This depends upon the work to which it yields, and you know that I have unceasingly insisted, as concerns the nonideal exteriority of writing, the gram, the trace, the text, etc., upon the necessity of never separating them from *work,* a value itself to be rethought outside its Hegelian affiliation. What is announced here, as I tried to indicate in *"La double séance"* (double science, double sense, double scene), is again the operation of the double mark or the re-mark. The concept of matter must be marked twice (the others too): in the deconstructed field[34]—this is the phase of overturning—and in the deconstructing text, outside the oppositions in which it has been caught (matter/spirit, matter/ideality, matter/form, etc.). By means of the play of this interval between the two marks, one can operate both an overturning deconstruction and a positively displacing, transgressive, deconstruction.

Rigorously reinscribed in the general economy (Bataille)[35] and in the double writing of which we were just speaking, the insistence on matter as the absolute exterior of opposition, the materialist insistence (in contact with what "materialism" has represented as a force of resistance in the history of philosophy) seems to me necessary. It is unequally necessary, varying with the sites, the strategic situations, the practical and theoretical points advanced. In a very *determined* field of the most current situation, it seems to me that the materialist insistence can function as a means of having the necessary generalization of the concept of text, its extension with no simple exterior limit (which also supposes the passage through metaphysical opposition), not wind up, (under the influence of very precise interests, reactive forces determined to lead work astray into confusion), not wind up, then, as the definition of a new self-interiority, a new "idealism," if you will, of the text. In effect, we must avoid having the indispensable critique of a certain naive relationship to the signified or the referent, to sense or meaning, remain fixed in a suspension, that is, a pure and simple suppression, of meaning or reference. I believe that I have taken precautions on this matter in the propositions that I have advanced. But it is true, and the proofs are not lacking, that this is never sufficient. What we need is to determine *otherwise,* according to a differential system, the *effects* of ideality, of signification, of meaning, and of reference. (We also would have to make room for a systematic analysis of the word "effect" which is used so frequently today—not an insignificant fact—and for the new concept which it marks in still rather undecided fashion. The frequency of this usage multiplies by virtue of this active indetermination. A concept in the process of constituting itself first produces a kind of localizable effervescence in the work of nomination. This "new" concept of *effect* borrows its characteristics from both the opposition cause/effect and from the opposition essence/appearance—*effect, reflect—without nevertheless being reduced to them*. It is this fringe of irreducibility that is to be analyzed.)

Of course we must redouble our prudence in reconsidering the problem of meaning and reference. The "dialectics" of the same and the other, of outside and inside, of the homogeneous and the heterogeneous, are, as you know, among the most *contorted* ones.[36] The outside can always become again an "object" in the polarity subject/object, or the reassuring reality of what is outside the text; and there is sometimes an "inside" that is as troubling as the outside may be reassuring. This is not to be overlooked in the critique of interiority and subjectivity.[37] Here we are in an extremely complex logic. The improvised speech of an interview cannot substitute for the textual work.

Houdebine: Your answer calls for the intervention of a question that we had anticipated for later, but which can be approached now. In the overall strategic regulation of your work, whose fundamental logic you have just recalled, notably as concerns the double mark (overturning, transgression of the deconstructed philosophical field), you effectively have been led to take into consideration a certain kind of textual work in relation to which one could pose the problem of the status of your own discourse. It is evident that in working on Mallarmé, on Artaud, on Bataille, on Sollers there is something unheard of in relationship to what classical philosophy has led us to expect: this is evidently not an aesthetic recreation, a commentary that redoubles a certain "poetic beauty," of the kind we have had repeated examples of in France. As a function of precisely everything that you have just delineated, and notably as concerns the necessity of the encounter with the materialist text, could you now define the relationship of your work to the textual work called "literary," which plays such an important role in your reflections?

Scarpetta: To accentuate the question that has just been asked: in a text like *"La dissémination"* you clearly mark Sollers's *practice,* both production and simultaneously what exceeds production, the practice of nonproduction, "an operation of annulation, of discount, and of a certain textual zero." What you mark here seems to me to be extremely important: Sollers's text, and the rupture it operates in a field of the signifier, "literature," is constituted on the basis of this double register of production and nonproduction, without it being possible to privilege one of the two terms over the other. I would like to know if a discourse like yours seems indebted to such a logic?

Derrida: I am tempted to answer very quickly: yes. In any case, this is what I would like to do. I have tried to describe and to explain how writing structurally carries within itself (counts-discounts) the process of its own erasure and annulation, all the while marking what *remains* of this erasure, according to a logic very difficult to summarize here. I would say that I have tried to do this more and more, according to a rule of increasing complexity, generalization, or accumulation that has not failed to provoke, as concerns the recent publications you mentioned, resistances or out-of-hand rejections even on the part of the best informed readers.

Yes, then, on the "double register." It remains that this did not *first* come up in the so-called literary field, but took support from texts belonging in a certain way to the "history of philosophy." What pushed me onto this route was the conviction that if one does not elaborate a general, theoretical, and systematic strategy of philosophical deconstruction, then textual irruptions always risk falling by the wayside into excess or empirical experimentation, and, sometimes simultaneously, into classical metaphysics. Now, this is what I wished to avoid. But I am not overlooking the fact that this *first* runs an inverse or symmetrical risk. Despite all the signs of prudence I have multiplied since the beginning of our discussion, I simply believe that certain risks must be run.

I cannot "talk" the writing or, as is said, the "composition" of the texts in question; this is the last thing that can be mastered in an interview. I will note only that the effects of the theoretical theses I have judged necessary to inscribe in these texts have often dissimulated the texts' texture; and inversely. This is completely deliberate on my part.

Yes, it is incontestable that certain texts classed as "literary" have seemed to me to operate breaches or infractions at the most advanced points. Artaud, Bataille, Mallarmé, Sollers. Why? At least for the reason that induces us to suspect the denomination "literature," and which subjects the concept to belles-lettres, to the arts, to poetry, to rhetoric, and to philosophy. These texts operate, in their very movement, the demonstration and practical deconstruction of the *representation* of what was done with literature, it being well understood that long before these "modern" texts a certain "literary" practice was able to operate against this model, against this representation. But it is on the basis of these last texts, on the basis of the general configuration to be remarked in them, that one can best reread, without retrospective teleology, the law of the previous fissures.

Thus, certain texts, and among them those to which you just alluded, seemed to me to mark and to organize a structure of resistance to the philosophical conceptuality that allegedly dominated or comprehended them, whether directly, or whether through categories derived from this philosophical fund, the categories of esthetics, rhetoric, or traditional criticism. For example the values of meaning or of content, of form or signifier, of metaphor/metonymy, of truth, of representation, etc., at least in their classical form, can no longer account for

certain very determined effects of these texts. This is
what I tried to bring out concerning Sollers's *Nombres*
(and his previous fictions) and Mallarmé's *"Mimique"*
(and an entire network of other texts); all of this resting
on the most general question of "truth" in its relationship to the also general question of "literariness." It
was, I believe, a decisive progress of this half-century to
have explicitly formulated the question of literarity, notably starting with the Russian formalists (not only starting with them: by virtue of an ensemble of historical
necessities, the most immediately determining one being
a certain transformation of literary practice itself). The
emergence of this question of literarity has permitted the
avoidance of a certain number of reductions and mis-
construings that always will have a tendency to reemerge
(thematism, sociologism, historicism, psychologism in all
their most disguised forms). Whence the necessity of formal and syntaxic work. Nevertheless, a symmetrical re-
action or reduction is now discernible: it consists in isolat-
ing, in order to shelter it, a formal specificity of the literary
which would have its own proper essence and truth
which would no longer have to be articulated with other
theoretical or practical fields. Whence the movement of
what I outlined in *"La double séance"*:[38] to mark a certain
wariness about the motif of "literarity" at the very moment of opposing it to the stubborn authority of the ensemble of what I name *mimetologism* (not *mimesis*, but a
determined interpretation of *mimesis*). Everything goes
through this chiasm, all writing is caught in it—practices
it. The form of the chiasm, of the *X*, interests me a great
deal, not as the symbol of the unknown, but because
there is in it, as I underline in *"La dissémination,"* a kind
of fork (the series *crossroads, quadrifurcum, grid, trellis,
key,* etc.) that is, moreover, unequal, one of the points
extending its range further than the other: this is the figure of the double gesture, the intersection, of which we
were speaking earlier.

Thus, to answer your questions, I will say that my texts belong neither to the "philosophical" register nor to the "literary" register. Thereby they communicate, or so I hope at least, with other texts that, having operated a certain rupture, can be called "philosophical" or "literary" only according to a kind of paleonomy: the question of *paleonomy:* what is the strategic necessity (and why do we still call *strategic* an operation that in the last analysis refuses to be governed by a teleo-eschatological horizon? Up to what point is this refusal possible and how does it *negotiate* its effects? Why must it negotiate these effects, including the effect of this *why* itself? Why does *strategy* refer to the *play* of the strategem rather than to the hierarchical organization of the means and the ends? etc. These questions will not be quickly reduced.), what, then, is the "strategic" necessity that requires the occasional maintenance of an *old name* in order to launch a new concept? With all the reservations imposed by this classical distinction between the name and the concept, one might begin to describe this operation. Taking into account the fact that a name does not name the punctual simplicity of a concept, but rather a system of predicates defining a concept, a conceptual structure *centered* on a given predicate, we proceed: (1) to the extraction of a reduced predicative trait that is held in reserve, limited in a given conceptual structure (limited for motivations and relations of force to be analyzed), *named X;* (2) to the delimitation, the grafting and regulated extension of the extracted predicate, the name X being maintained as a kind of *lever of intervention,* in order to maintain a grasp on the previous organization, which is to be transformed effectively. Therefore, extraction, graft, extension: you know that this is what I call, according to the process I have just described, *writing.*

Houdebine: Let us go back then, according to the constellationlike form of our itinerary, to a problem already posed in a preceding question, and which is re-posed of

itself concerning the question of the "old name." From
what you have just formulated I will retain that it is quite
accurate that the materialist text, in the history of its repression, has not been sheltered from the dangers implied by every form of simply overturning the dominant
idealist discourse; this materialist discourse thereby can
take on a metaphysical form (that is, a mechanistic, non-
dialectical form), remaining prisoner of the oppositional
couples of the dominant (idealist, metaphysical) discourse, couples within which this materialist discourse
can overturn idealist, metaphysical discourse according
to a known tactic, that is, according to a gesture that this
(mechanistic) materialism cannot thoroughly master.

But, as you yourself indicated, in the itinerary of a
strategy this overturning *is not nothing* (it is not
exhausted by a purely specular relationship), and its result (like the result of every process of contradiction) "is
not equal to zero"; this overturning "which is not nothing" itself being caught in a history, the differentiated
history of materialism and dialectics, in which is implied
necessarily the articulation, and authority, of politics over
ideology.

Further, it is a fact that in its dialectical form, such as it
was elaborated most notably from Marx to Lenin, after
Hegel, the materialist text cannot be reduced to the
underside of an (idealist) position within one and the
same metaphysical couple, but on the contrary, as Sollers
indicated in *"Lénine et le materialisme philosophique"* (*Tel
Quel*, no. 43), is in a *dyssemmetrical* position in relation to
the idealist discourse whose linear coupling it *exceeds*.

In order to approach one aspect of our discussion, and
notably on the terrain of the question of the "old names,"
do you not think that you can say about the concept of
contradiction what you say about the concept of the *unconscious* when you are led to determine the Freudian unconscious as the mark of an "alterity" that is "definitively

exempt from every process of presentation by means of which we would call on it to show itself in person," and that thereby, if Freud gives this "alterity" "the metaphysical name of the unconscious," the concept so designated, such as it functions in the economy of Freudian theory and practice, escapes, in its strict meaning, a metaphysical reduction; is it not the same, then, for *contradiction*: a "metaphysical name," if one thinks of its inscription in Hegelian dialectics to the extent that the latter may be considered overdetermined by the teleological movement of the *Aufhebung;* but what the concept so named designates, in the economy of a materialist dialectics, has nothing in common, in its strict meaning, with metaphysical discourse; for perhaps we would still have to discuss the appellation "metaphysical name" for the concept of contradiction, including its Hegelian inscription: (a) because an entire metaphysical line of thought (logocentrist, in effect) has presented itself, and continues to present itself, explicitly as a suppression-repression of contradiction, a repression-suppression that Hegelian dialectics, in a very important historical gesture, breaks and opens (on what is suppressed-repressed) according to a movement whose historical point of overturning is constituted by dialectical materialism, which *also* displaces it onto another terrain; (b) because contradiction, the reflection of contradiction, is indeed the fundamental motif of a materialist text ideologically and politically suppressed-repressed for centuries, the difficulties of whose elaboration (already mentioned) should not make us forget that in its dialectical ground it *exceeds* metaphysical discourse (not being thoroughly caught in it) in the extent to which what has been called "spirit" or "consciousness" is conceived by materialism as one of the forms of matter (since Lucretius, for example, spoke of the "corporal nature of the soul and the spirit"), which itself is fundamentally determined, as a philosophical concept, by its "'unique' property," as Lenin says, "of *being an objective reality*, of existing outside our consciousness," or, to return to a recent statement operating in the field of a dialectical materialist analysis of the signifying practices, as that which "is not meaning," that "which is without meaning, outside and despite it" (Kristeva), this radical heterogeneity (matter/meaning) by the same token defining itself "as the field of contradiction."

But doubtless we would have to ask you to specify what the status of *"différance,"* and the logic it implies, might be in relation to *contradiction*, which as we might recall, in order to permit the leap into other questions, Kristeva defined in the same text (*"Matière, sens, dialectique,"* Tel Quel 44) as "the matrix of signifying."

Derrida: Here I cannot give you an answer in principle different from the one I gave concerning the concept of "matter." I do not believe that there is any "fact" which permits us to say: in *the* Marxist text, contradiction *itself*, dialectics *itself* escapes from *the* dominance of metaphysics. Further, you speak, citing Lenin, of the "unique property" of "being an objective reality, of existing outside our consciousness." Each element of this proposition, you must recognize, poses serious problems. Here one must investigate all the sediments deposited by the history of metaphysics. If, in the last analysis, and solely in this form, this proposition governed Lenin's philosophical text, it would not be the one to convince me of a break with metaphysics. Now, wherever, and in the extent to which, the motif of contradiction functions effectively, in a textual work, outside speculative dialectics, and taking into account a new problematic of meaning (can one say that this problematic is elaborated in Marx and in Lenin? And would it be anti-Marxist to doubt it? Aren't there enough historical reasons to explain this, to justify it?) I agree. Don't you see, once

again, I do not believe that one can speak, even from a
Marxist point of view, of a homogeneous Marxist text
that would instantaneously liberate the concept of contradiction from its speculative, teleological, and
eschatological horizon. If, from this point of view, one
wishes to relocate what you have called the "repressed"
of philosophy, and notably as concerns matter and contradiction, one must not only go back to Marx, or at least
to an entire stratum of the text he opened up, but much
further back, as Marx himself knew, as far as the "Greek
materialists," traversing problems of reading and "translation" that are indeed difficult, and whose results are
difficult to anticipate in our lexicon. Here, in a certain
way, we are at the bare beginnings. (In *"La double
séance"* I limited myself to several discreet references to
Democrites' *"rhythmos"*—both writing and rhythm—an
important term, it appears, in a system that Plato doubtless wished to reduce to silence by "ontologizing" it.)[39]
For as long as this work, which supposes an immense
and meticulous itinerary of reading, has not been done,
and it will take a great deal of time, this field will remain
in a state of fundamental indetermination. Not that an
entire scientific process can be hung on one philological
discovery. But the strategic choice of signifiers (what we
are debating about here) cannot be entirely independent
of these historical readings.

Houdebine: I feel that I am entirely in agreement with
you on this point, and I would never think of alleging
that there is a completely homogeneous Marxist text as
concerns the concept of contradiction. I was only won-
dering whether one could consider that in every materialist stand [*prise de position*], at its heart (and this is why
I recalled Lucretius's line marking the "corporal nature of
the soul and the spirit"), and inscribed in a structurally
necessary way, one finds the double motif of "matter"
and "contradiction"; which led me to pose anew, but

from another angle, the question of the relationship between the logic derived from the double register
"matter/contradiction" and the logic implied by the motif
of *différance:* a relationship rendered necessary by the fact
that, as you have emphasized, your work can be conceived as a critique of idealism; and a question also necessary in the extent to which the two kinds of logic in
question do not completely overlap. For example, can you
currently conceive in your work, which you develop on
the basis of an economy in which the concept of contradiction does not appear, of the possibility of a relationship to the economy implied in the motif "matter/
contradiction"?

Derrida: The concept of contradiction does not occupy
the foreground for the reasons I have just indicated (relationship to Hegel: "The fellow demands time to be di-
gested," Engels, speaking of Hegel; letter to C. Schmidt,
1 November 1891). But as for the kernel, or rather the
interval which constitutes the concept and the effects of
contradiction (*différance* and conflict, etc.) what I have
written seems to me entirely explicit.

Houdebine: Perhaps then we could further specify the
meaning of our question by asking it in a more precise
field.

Scarpetta: In *"La parole soufflée"* [in *Writing and Difference*], for example, you speak of Artaud's relationship
to metaphysics; you emphasize that Artaud simultaneously solicits the system of metaphysics and at the
same time shakes it, destroys it, exceeds it in his practice.
Does not this practice of shaking, of excess, of destruction seem to you to derive from a logic of contradiction,
released from its speculative investments?

Derrida: Yes, why not? Provided that one determines
the concept of contradiction with the necessary critical
precautions, and by elucidating its relationship or non-
relationship to Hegel's *Logic.* This is very quickly said, of

course. (I speak of contradiction and dialectics in one of the texts on Artaud.)[40]

Houdebine: Since we have been led to speak of Hegel again, perhaps this would be the moment to have another question intervene, overlapping with the previous question about the relationship between your work and the "literary" text, that is, a certain kind of signifying function. I am thinking notably of your study *"Le puits et la pyramide (introduction à la sémiologie de Hegel)"*: what makes Hegel's text particularly fascinating, among other things, is that one finds in it both the process of the "reappropriation of meaning" brought to its highest degree of dialectical complexity (which leads you to write in *Of Grammatology:* "Hegel, the last philosopher of the Book"), and also the practice of a signifying logic that is attentive to its own inscription in language, on the stage of language (and you add: Hegel, "first thinker of writing"). In relation to Hegel, then, what do you think must be attributed to the process of Hegelian dialectics as such? And if in relation to Hegel you operate in "infinitesimal and radical displacement," do you do so by passage to a completely exterior terrain (but he is the "first thinker of writing"), and if not, what aspect of Hegelianism could constitute for you what the Marxist text has called the "rational kernel" of Hegelian dialectics?

Derrida: To answer in an immediate fashion I will say: never on a totally, or simply, exterior terrain. But your question is very difficult. We will never be finished with the reading or rereading of Hegel, and, in a certain way, I do nothing other than attempt to explain myself on this point. In effect I believe that Hegel's text is necessarily fissured; that it is something more and other than the circular closure of its representation. It is not reduced to a content of philosophemes, it also necessarily produces a powerful writing operation, a remainder of writing, whose

strange relationship to the philosophical content of
Hegel's text must be reexamined, that is, the movement
by means of which his text exceeds its meaning, permits
itself to be turned away from, to return to, and to repeat
itself outside its self-identity. On this question one can
find very interesting, though doubtless insufficient, indications in Feuerbach, who at least posed the problem of
Hegel the *writer*, of a certain *contradiction* (Feuerbach's
word) between Hegel's writing and his "system." I cannot engage myself any further on this question now, but I
will do so in a text to appear this winter.

In all this, the entire question of the "rational kernel"
(are these the terms in which this question is to be formulated today? I am not sure) cannot be elaborated, in
effect, except by passage, *in particular*, through Marx's
Engels's, Lenin's readings of Marx; among other texts,
Lenin's *Notebooks on Dialectics* which deserve a textual
scrutiny, a specific kind of reading, that could not be
attempted up to now, and which now becomes more accessible. (This is the principle of your text in *Théorie d'ensemble*, of Soller's and Christine Glucksmann's texts on
Lenin in *Tel Quel*, and generally speaking, of the works
of the *Tel Quel* group—an occasion for me to recall a solidarity and support regularly kept up, as you know, for
five or six years.) What is Lenin doing when he writes,
across from a Hegelian statement, "read!" (interpret?
transform? translate? understand?)? Follow too, all the
"metaphors" by means of which Lenin tries to determine
the relationship of dialectical materialism to Hegelian
logic, "metaphors" that at first sight are incompatible
("genius," "foresight," and "system," overturning and
decapitation, genetic or organic development of the
"seed" or the "germ"). Taken one by one these
metaphors would be insufficient, but in their active
"contradiction" they produce quite an other effect. There

are many more of them,[41] and this profusion of written
figures, each of which, on its own, sometimes refers to a
point still within Hegel, but which mutually set each
other off, opens up the practical and theoretical question
of a new definition of the relationship between the logic
of dialectical materialism and Hegelian logic. It also contributes to the general reexamination of the historical
space that I will call in shorthand the *after-Hegel*, and at
the same time contributes to the new questions on writing, philosophical writing, the scene of writing and philosophy. This can be done only by reinscribing these
texts in the force of their writing, and by posing the
problem, for the field we are concerned with, of Lenin's
language, of the historical field in which he wrote, of the
precise situation and the political strategy that govern the
formation of his texts, etc.

  Houdebine: This doubtless leads us to ask other questions. All along your itinerary you have been led to take
support, for example through a reading of texts like those
of Mallarmé or Artaud, but also throughout the *Grammatology*, from a concept like that of the *signifier*, a concept proposed by linguistics, and that you strategically
reinscribe in another chain (*différance*/writing/trace), a
chain in which the signifier is situated in a dependent
position. A complex dependence, however, since within
the concept of the signifier there is also marked, as in
your text itself, another chain which cannot be reduced
(at least in my opinion) to the first: exteriority-
heterogeneity of the signifier (you also speak of the *body*,
of a "writing of the body") in relation to the direct grasp
of the signified according to the classical theme of
metaphysics in the immediate proximity of self to self in
consciousness. In this way, to the motif of *différance* as
the "possibility of conceptuality, of the conceptual process and system in general," is necessarily joined an-

other motif by means of which this "possibility" itself is determined as never referring to a transcendental ego (the unity of an "I think"), but on the contrary as inscribing itself in what is radically exterior to the subject, which "becomes a *speaking* subject only in commerce with the system of linguistic differences," or again "becomes a *signifier* (in general, in speech or any other sign) only by inscribing itself in the system of differences." Further, these "differences," you say too, have not "fallen from the sky," are "no more inscribed in a *topos noetos* than prescribed in the wax of the brain"; "from the outset," they would even be "thoroughly historical," "if the word 'history' did not bear within it the motif of a final repression of difference."

There are several questions to ask then: (a) What about these "differences" which, in effect, have not "fallen from the sky"? What can the "playing movement which produces [them]" designate, as concerns "history" that in the last analysis is contested as the "final repression of difference," if one recalls that the motif of *heterogeneity* cannot be conceived only within the theme of spacing, in the extent to which the motif of heterogeneity implies the double moment (the movement of a contradiction) of a *difference* (void, spacing) and the *position* of an *alterity*. Can one not think that these "differences," here as linguistic differences, linguistic signifiers, still derive from what Lacan calls the *symbolic*, and that they therefore are essentially linked (and not only in a factual fashion, as a phenomenal deviation from a "*différance*" or "playing movement which produces [them]"), to *social practice* in the aspect of its signifying means of production (its languages)? (b) Whence, a second question: what relationship does a problematic of writing seem to you to maintain to the problematic of the signifier such as Lacan has developed it, in which the signifier "represents the subject for another signifier"?

Derrida: First of all I do not see very clearly why the notion of spacing, at least as I practice it, is incompatible with the motif of heterogeneity...

Houdebine: No, that is not what I said: let me rephrase the question: is the motif of heterogeneity entirely covered by the notion of spacing? Do not *alterity* and *spacing* present us with two moments not identical to each other?

Derrida: In effect, these two concepts *do not signify exactly* the same thing; that being said, I believe that they are absolutely indissociable.

Houdebine: Entirely so; I said in the preliminaries to my question that they were dialectically, that is contradictorally linked.

Derrida: Spacing designates *nothing,* nothing that is, no presence at a distance; it is the index of an irreducible exterior, and at the same time of a *movement,* a displacement that indicates an irreducible alterity. I do not see how one could dissociate the two concepts of spacing and alterity.

Houdebine: Permit me to repeat: it is in no way a question of dissociating these two concepts. If you wish, let us make the impact of this question appear in a more precise field, indicated in what I just asked: that of the status of these differences which "have not fallen from the sky," of these linguistic differences...

Derrida: Not only linguistic...

Houdebine: In effect; but spacing as such, in its strict acceptance, in my opinion, cannot by itself, *for example,* account for the system of linguistic differences in which a subject is called upon to constitute itself.

Derrida: Indeed. It is evident that the concept of spacing, by itself, cannot account for anything, any more than any other concept. It cannot account for the differences—the different things—between which is opened the spacing which nevertheless delimits them. But it would be to accord a theological function to this concept to expect it to be an explicating principle of all determined spaces, of all different things. Spacing certainly operates in all fields, but precisely as different fields. And its operation is different each time, articulated otherwise.[42]

As for my occasional recourse to the concept of the *signifier*, it is also deliberately equivocal. Double inscription again. (The *incision* of deconstruction, which is not a voluntary decision or an absolute beginning, does not take place just anywhere, or in an absolute elsewhere. An incision, precisely, it can be made only according to lines of force and forces of rupture that are localizable in the discourse to be deconstructed. The *topical* and *technical* determination of the most necessary sites and operators—beginnings, holds, levers, etc.—in a given situation depends upon an historical analysis. This analysis is *made* in the general movement of the field, and is never exhausted by the conscious calculation of a "subject.") On the one hand, the signifier is a positive lever: thus I define writing as the impossibility of a chain arresting itself on a signified that would not relaunch this signified, in that the signified is already in the position of the signifying substitution. In this phase of overturning, one *opposes,* insistently, the pole of the signifier to the dominant authority of the signified. But this necessary overturning is also insufficient, and I will not elaborate further. Thus I have regularly marked the turn by means of which the word "signifier" leads us back to or retains us in the logocentric circle.[43]

As for the other aspect of the same question, which concerns a specific and difficult text, I will attempt to explain myself, at least briefly, in an indicative and programmatic mode. Here too, whether it is a question of the discourse of psychoanalysis in general, or of Lacan's discourse, nothing is given, or functions as a homogeneous given.

I have already told you what I think about the notion of the signifier. The same holds for the notions of *representation* and *subject*.

To come to the point, without undue length (*"La double séance"* is precisely a treatment of the point, of length, of castration, and of dissemination), but without skipping over a question that cannot be reduced to these three conceptual atoms, to come to the point, then, about what my "position" might be on the question, is it entirely useless to recall first that since *Of Grammatology* (1965) and "Freud and the Scene of Writing" (1966; in *Writing and Difference*) *all* my texts have inscribed what I will call their psychoanalytic import? From which it does not follow that all the previous texts did not also do so ("Force and Signification," "Violence and Metaphysics," *"La parole soufflée,"* etc. [all in *Writing and Difference*]). The question, then, is asked each time. Explicitly, purposely asked, but also while bearing in mind, *in the writing itself and in the handling of concepts,* the *determined* blank or playing space imposed by the *still to come* theoretical articulation of the new general question of the gram—and of the specificity of each text (a question that then becomes effervescent)—with the question of psychoanalysis. In each text, as can be verified, I constrain myself to act such that in relation to this indispensable articulation, what I consider to be *new* theoretical and practical premises do not in advance close off the problematic, are not muddled by hasty interferences having no rigorous status, in brief, that they maintain a form such that in principle they will not be disqualified by eventual results (which of course *always* remains possible: which is why I said "I constrain myself." And, even if said in passing, this framework is also valid, *mutatis mutandis,* for the relationship of grammatology to Marxism). The issue, then, in undertaking, practically and theoretically, these new modes of articulation, was to fracture a still quite hermetic closure: the closure that shelters the question of writing (in general, and notably philosophical and literary writing) from psychoanalysis, but equally the closure that so frequently blinds psychoanalytic discourse to a certain structure of the textual scene.

Today then, I can see a working program delineate itself, from my point of view, and insofar as I can anticipate, in the field of *"La dissémination"* (in the text that bears that title, and of which it precipitously could be said that its explicit "themes" are the column, the cut, the blow, the hymen, and castration, in their relationship to the *two,* the *four,* to a certain Oedipal trinity, to dialectics, to the *relève,* to the "east," to presence, etc., and to the set of questions that interested me elsewhere), in *"La pharmacie de Platon"* (same remark) and in *"La double séance"* (more directly in the import of notes 8, 9, 10, 53, 55, 61, etc., but *in practice* everywhere). As appears in these texts, and in *"La mythologie blanche,"* for those who are willing to read, the most general title of the problem would be: castration and mimesis. Here I can only refer to these analyses and their consequences.

In effect, in these analyses the concept of castration is indissociable from that of dissemination. But dissemination situates the *more or less* that indefinitely resists—and equally situates that which resists against—the effect of subjectivity, of subjectivation, of appropriation (*relève,* sublimation, idealization, reinteriorization [*Erinnerung*], signification, semantization, autonomy, law, etc.), what Lacan calls—I am answering your question—the order of the "symbolic." Escapes it and disorganizes it, makes it drift, marks its writing, with all the implied risks, but without letting itself be conceived in the categories of the "imaginary" or the "real." I have never been convinced of the necessity of this conceptual tripartition. It is pertinent only *within* the system that I put into question.[44] If

you truly wish to investigate it from this particular point
of view, dissemination would be not only the possibility
for a mark to "disembed" itself (see the play on this clinical[45] word in *"La pharmacie de Platon," "La dissémination,"* and *"La double séance"*), not only the force—the
force of repetition, and therefore of automaticity *and*
exportation—which permits it to break what fastens it to
the unity of a signified that would not be without it, not
only the possibility of bursting from this *clasp,* and of
undoing the eider quilt of the "symbolic" (I believe that I
am citing a seldom quoted passage from Lautréamont on
the *eider,* I will have to check). It is also the possibility of
deconstructing (such is the general opening of a
practical-theoretical deconstruction, which is not in-
vented one fine day), or, if you prefer, of unsewing (this
is the "unsew-it" of *"La pharmacie de Platon"*) the symbolic order in its general structure *and* in its modifications, in the general *and* determined forms of sociality,
the "family" or culture. The effective violence of disseminating writing. An infraction *marking* the "symbolic." Would every possibility of disorder and disor-
ganization in the symbolic, from the vantage of a
certain outside force, would everything that *forces* the
symbolic, derive from the specular (or the "imaginary"),
that is, from a "real" determined as the "impossible"?
From schizophrenia or psychosis? In this case, what are
the conclusions to be drawn?[46] This is the breach that
interests me under the rubric of dissemination.

I am not saying that the "symbolic" (to continue to use
a word whose choice has always perplexed me) *does not in
fact constitute itself,* does not constitute the solidity of an
order (it is also the order of philosophy), and that it is not
structurally called upon to constitute and reconstitute itself unceasingly (language, law, "intersubjective triad,"
"intersubjective dialectics," speaking truth, etc.). But
dissemination designates that which can no more be

integrated into the symbolic than it can form the symbolic's *simple* exterior under the heading of its failure or
its (imaginary or real) impossibility: even if, from the
padded interior of the "symbolic," it is in one's interest
to be taken in by its tricky *resemblance* to these two forms.
What is overlooked, then, is perhaps not fiction (and this
concept still would have to be analyzed), but simulacrum:
a structure of duplicity that plays and doubles the dual
relationship, interrupts more efficaciously, more "really"
(it is measured by its reactive effects), both the specular
(to be rethought in this case) or the proper, and the
"symbolic," a structure of duplicity that can no longer be
mastered in a problematic of speech, of the lie and truth.
Effective violence and *unconscious* effects of the simulacrum.

Lapidarily: dissemination figures that which *cannot be*
the father's.[47] Neither in germination nor in castration.
Try to control the turns of this proposition, and on the
way, while walking [*en marchant*], you will find (mark)
and lose (margin) the limit between polysemia and
dissemination.

To write—dissemination: is this not to take into account castration (with its entire system, and according to
the strange arithmetic you mentioned just now) by once
more putting at stake its position as a signified or transcendental signifier (for there can also be a transcendental
signifier, for example the phallus as the correlate of a
primary signified, castration and the mother's desire),[48]
the ultimate recourse of all textuality, the central truth, or
truth in the last analysis, the semantically full and non-
substitutable definition of the generating (disseminating)
void in which the text is launched? Dissemination *affirms*
(I do not say produces or controls) endless substitution, it
neither arrests nor controls play ("Castration—in play
always . . .").[49] And in doing so, runs all the risks, but
without the metaphysical or romantic pathos of negativ-
ity. Dissemination "is" this *angle* of the play of castration

which does not signify, which permits itself to be constituted neither as a signified, nor a signifier, no more
presents than represents itself, no more shows than hides
itself. Therefore in and of itself it is neither truth (ade-
quation or unveiling) nor veil. It is what I have called the
graphic of the hymen, which can no longer be measured
by the opposition veil/nonveil.[50]

Scarpetta: I would like to ask you then what relationship you establish between dissemination and the
death instinct?

Derrida: The most necessary relationship. On the basis
of *Beyond the Pleasure Principle* and *"Das Unheimliche"*[51]
(whose byways are extraordinarily difficult), and on the
basis of everything tied to them in the previous and future texts, we must reconstitute a logic that in many respects seems to contradict, or in any case to complicate
singularly, Freud's entire explicit and "regional" discourse on "literature" and "art." I have often referred,
particularly in *"La différance"* and *"La double séance,"* to
the "death instinct," to a certain dualism, and to a certain
concept of repetition to be found in the two texts I just
mentioned. All of this calls for (this is what I am working
on now) an elaboration which relates a new concept of
repetition (which is at work, but discontinuously, in
Freud) to the value of *mimesis* (and not, of course,
mimetologism, representation, expression, imitation,
illustration, etc.).

Scarpetta: This could lead us to articulate another
question on what might be called the "subject of writing"; for example, in the extent to which you mark that
the "subject of writing" does not exist, if one understands by this expression a master-subject, and that by
"subject of writing" one must understand the system of
relationships between textual layers themselves, how
could one return to this problem of the "subject of writing" on the basis of the concept of dissemination, and
return to it on the basis of what is articulated in this con-

cept, that is, the dialectic between sublimation and the death instinct?

Derrida: As you recall, I have never said that *there is not* a "subject of writing."[52] After the questions asked on the occasion of the lecture on *"La différance"*[53] I was led to recall this to Goldmann, who also was quite worried about the subject, and about where it had gone. It is solely necessary to reconsider the problem of the effect of subjectivity such as it is produced by the structure of the text. The problem of what I designated just now as the "general text"—its "block"[54]—and not only of the linguistic text. Doubtless this effect is inseparable from a certain relationship between sublimation and the death instinct, from a movement of interiorization-idealization-*relève*-sublimation, etc., and therefore from a certain repression. And it would be ridiculous to overlook the necessity of this chain, and even more so to raise some moral or political "objection" to it. Without it, in effect, there would be neither "subject," nor "history," nor the "symbolic," etc. Nor could these exist by virtue of this chain alone, moreover. Thus we would have to reexamine all these concepts in terms of what more and more clearly appears to be their concantenation, not their overlapping or identity. I can say no more while improvising, unless you make your question more specific.

Scarpetta: For example, must one admit a radical cleavage between the "subject of writing" and what Lacan calls "subject," as the "effect of the signifier," as produced in and by the signifier, or, on the contrary, can or should these two notions encounter each other?

Derrida: Certainly there is a "relationship" between these two definitions of the "subject." To analyze it, in any case, we would have to keep track of what was said just now about dissemination and the "symbolic," the gram and the signifier, etc.

Houdebine: One last question, if you will, which is articulated over the development of the entirety of your work. You write, in one of your first published texts, "Freud and the Scene of Writing" (1966; *Tel Quel*, no. 26), contesting the pretentions of a sociology of literature— and we are in complete agreement with you—that "the sociality of writing as drama requires a totally other discipline."

Today, how would you determine this "totally other discipline"? What relationship would the latter maintain with a semiotics and a semanalysis developing on the dialectical materialist logical basis? Which is necessarily to ask, as a final prolongation, the question of the relationship between the "concept" of writing and the Marxist concept of practice, and singularly of signifying practice, such as it may be constituted as the object of knowledge, precisely, in a semiotics and a semanalysis based on a dialectical materialist logic, which is equally determined on the basis of an intervention of psychoanalysis, an intervention that is absolutely necessary as soon as one takes on the field of the signifying practices.

But doubtless we would also have to speak of the retroaction of the modern text on the procedures of analysis themselves, of what is implied, in contemporary textual practice, as *excess* in relation to a certain knowledge-gathering, scientific, logic.

Last aspect of the question, perhaps opening on a kind of provisional conclusion to this interview: how do you conceive, today, both the ensemble of this process (which is very difficult to think of, other than in the form of a contradictory, dialectical process), and its efficacity on the current ideological scene? What is it capable of transforming, what are its possible limits, its future?

Derrida: In the sentence you cited, "drama" was a citation, as you recognized, and even a double one.

Let us take off, for example, from the concept of practice. In order to define writing, the gram, *différance*, the text, etc., I have always insisted on the value *practice*.

Consequently, everywhere, from this point of view, that a general theory, a general theoretical-practice of the "signifying practices" is elaborated, I have always sub- scribed to the task thus defined. I suppose that you are referring to the works of Julia Kristeva.

It is also evident that in the field of a deconstruction of philosophical oppositions, the opposition *praxis/theoria* first is to be analyzed, and may no longer simply govern our definition of practice. For this reason too, systematic deconstruction cannot be a simply theoretical or simply negative operation. We must be on guard indefinitely against the "reappropriation" of the value "practice."

Now what can the "efficacity" of all this work, all this deconstructive practice, be on the "contemporary ideological scene"? Here I can only respond in principle and mark a point. This work *seems* to take its point of departure from limited fields, defined as the fields of "ideology" (philosophy, science, literature, etc.). There- fore, there seem to be no grounds for expecting from it an immoderate historical efficacity, an *immediately general* efficacity. Efficacity, in order to be certain, remains no less relayed, articulated, or deferred, according to com- plex networks. But inversely, what is perhaps in the pro- cess of being reconsidered, is the form of closure that was called "ideology" (doubtless a concept to be analyzed in its function, its history, its origins, its transformations), the form of the relationships between a transformed con- cept of "infrastructure," if you will—an "infrastructure" of which the *general text* would no longer be an effect or a reflection[55]—and the transformed concept of "ideology." If what is in question in this work is a new definition of the relationship of a *determined* text or signifying chain to its exterior, to its referential effects, etc. (see above), to "reality" (history, class struggle, relationships of produc- tion, etc.), then we can no longer restrict ourselves to prior delimitations, nor even to the prior concept of a regional delimitation.[56] What is produced in the current trembling is a reevaluation of the relationship between the general text and what was believed to be, in the form of reality (history, politics, economics, sexuality, etc.), the simple, referable exterior of language or writing, the belief that this exterior could operate from the simple position of cause or accident. What are apparently simply "regional" effects of this trembling, therefore, at the same time have a nonregional opening, destroying their own limits and tending to articulate themselves with the general scene, but in new modes, without any pretention to mastery.

Fragment of a Letter from Jean-Louis Houdebine to Jacques Derrida

July 1, 1971

At heart, the underlying question of this exchange is the question of *materialism,* both as an overturning and as a displacement outside the field of classical philosophy; that is, the question of a materialist position [*prise de position*]. Doubtless this is the moment to recall Lenin's succinct, provocative formula (a scandal, for philosophy); the question of *taking a position* [*prise de position*] in philosophy. In effect, once more taking up the thread of our discussion: everything derives from my question on the motif of *heterogeneity,* a motif that I think is irreducible to the single motif of spacing. That is, the motif of heterogeneity indeed implies, in my opinion, the two moments of *spacing* and of *alterity,* moments that are in effect indissociable, but that are also not to be identified with each other, moments whose indissociability is that of a dialectical (materialist) contradiction. Why? Because if, as you say, *effectively* "spacing designates *nothing,* nothing that is, no presence at a distance, but is the index of an

irreducible exterior, and, simultaneously, of a movement, a displacement that indicates an absolutely irreducible alterity"—it remains that the motif of
heterogeneity is not reduced to, is not exhausted by
this "index of an irreducible exterior." It is *also the position of this alterity as such,* that is, the position of a
"something" (a "nothing") that *is not nothing* (and this
is why the motif of heterogeneity is the motif of a—of
the?—basic dialectical materialist contradiction:
"spacing/alterity") which all the while exceeds, in
principle, any reappropriation-interiorization-
idealization-*relève* in a becoming of Meaning, (no *Aufhebung* here), which would erase, would reduce the
very heterogeneity marked in it according to its own
double movement (spacing/alterity). That this "something" (this "nothing") "which is not nothing" can in
no way be subsumed by any "presence" whatever, is
what is marked—following the inverse trajectory of the
dialectical movement of contradiction—in the inscription of spacing; but, at the same time, this inscription
of spacing is supported only by what it negates in the
form of "presence" (and which indeed is, in fact, a
"nonpresence"): other, body, matter. The complete
development of the motif of heterogeneity thus obliges
us to go on to the positivity of this "nothing" designated by spacing that is always also a "something" (a
"nothing") "that is not nothing" (the *position* of irreducible alterity).

On the other hand, I agree with you that the problems you indicate can always reemerge on the basis of
this other-position: this is why the moment of spacing
(which is fundamental in the field circumscribed here,
the order of language and of the inscription of the constitution of the subject, which occurs according to an
irreducible cleavage) is essential. But not less essential
is the *other* moment, the moment of alterity (*position* of
alterity), whose logic I very cursorily attempted to define, since it is on this basis (the indissociability of
"spacing/alterity," which constitutes the materialist

motif *par excellence,* heterogeneity) that the theme of
the "differences" which have not "fallen from the sky"
can be inscribed, in its necessary articulation with the
entirety of a differentiated social practice (that is, both
in the aspect of its languages and in all its other
aspects—economic practice, political practice—which
although never confined to some extralinguistic
sector—language is not a superstructure—are none
the less practices irreducible to the single register of
language).

That *this* is stupefying, scandalous, as concerns the
entirety of a philosophy founded on the illusory reappropriation of alterity in the different forms of
idealism (metaphysics, spiritualism, formalist
positivism), is indeed what motivates Lenin to speak
of a "position": for philosophy, every materialist position derives from a veritable show of force supported
by the irreducible double buttress marked in the motif
of heterogeneity (spacing/alterity). And I think that
one could find not only in Lenin, but also in Bataille,
not a few developments along these lines.

Fragment of a letter from Jacques Derrida to Jean-Louis
Houdebine

July 15, 1971

We agree, then, about the *overturning/displacement.*

1. *Taking a position in philosophy:* nothing "shocks"
me less, of course.

Why engage in a work of deconstruction, rather than
leave things the way they are, etc.? Nothing here,
without a "show of force" somewhere. Deconstruction, I have insisted, is not *neutral.* It *intervenes.* I am
not sure that the imperative of taking a position in
philosophy has so regularly been considered "scandalous" in the history of metaphysics, whether one con-
siders this position-taking to be implicit or declared.

Nor am I sure—but here I suppose that we agree—that taking a position, at least as a show of force or as a force of rupture with the norms of traditional philosophical discourse, is essential to *every* materialism, to *materialism as such.* Are we agreed also that there is no *effective* and *efficient* position, no veritable force of rupture, without a minute, rigorous, extended analysis, an analysis that is as differentiated and as scientific as possible? Analysis of the greatest number of possible givens, and of the most diverse givens (general economy)? And that it is necessary to uproot this notion of taking a position from every determination that, in the last analysis, remains psychologistic, subjectivistic, moral and voluntaristic?

2. *Spacing/alterity:* on their indissociability, then, there is no disagreement between us. I have always underlined at least two characteristics in the analysis of spacing, as I recalled in the course of the interview: (1) That spacing is the impossibility for an identity to be closed on itself, on the inside of its proper interiority, or on its coincidence with itself. The irreducibility of spacing is the irreducibility of the other. (2) That "spacing" designates not only interval, but a "productive," "genetic," "practical" movement, an "operation," if you will, in its Mallarméan sense also. The irreducibility of the other is marked in spacing in relation to what you seem to designate by the notion of "position": in relation to our discussion of the other day, this is the newest and most important point, it seems to me, and I will come back to it in an instant.

Five remarks in the interval:

First: Is it not rather *new* to define the system of *spacing/alterity*, on which we agree, as an essential and indispensable mechanism of dialectical materialism?

Second: "No *Aufhebung* here," you write. I do not say this to take you at your word, but rather to underline the necessity of reinscription rather than denial: there is always *Aufhebung* (as there is always repression, idealization, sublimation, etc.).

Third: I would not subscribe unreservedly to what you say, at least in these terms, in the sentence: "this inscription of spacing is supported only by what it negates in the form of a 'presence' (and which is indeed, in fact, a 'nonpresence'): other, body, matter." I fear, precisely, that the category of "negation" reintroduces the Hegelian logic of the *Aufhebung*. It has happened that I have spoken of nonpresence, in effect, but by this I was designating less a negated presence, than "something" (nothing, indeed, in the form of presence) that deviates from the opposition presence/absence (negated presence), with all that this opposition implies. But this is too difficult a problem to take at the words of a letter. In the same sentence, do you think that *body* and *matter* always designate nonpresences in the same way as *other*? No more than it is a form of presence, *other* is not a *being* (a determined being, existence, essence, etc.).

Fourth: Without wishing to take you at your words, but again in order to specify what I think about spacing: I would not contend, for obvious reasons (in any event I would not literally contend this), that spacing is a *"moment"* and an "essential moment." Again, this is what is at stake in the relation to Hegel.

Fifth: I agree as concerns Bataille (see *Writing and Difference* p. 337, note 33).

Position (of alterity): taking into account point 2 (above in my letter), there is no disagreement between us, and, as I said in the interview, I cannot receive your insistence on this point as an addition or an objection to what I have written. Why, then, does it appear to me that the word "position" has to be handled prudently?

1. If the alterity of the other is *posed,* that is, *only* posed, does it not amount to *the same,* for example in the form of the "constituted object" or of the "informed product" invested with meaning, etc.? From this point of view, I would even say that the alterity of the other *inscribes* in this relationship that which in no

case can be "posed." Inscription, as I would define it in this respect, is not a simple position: it is rather that by means of which every position is *of itself confounded (différance)*: inscription, mark, text and not only *thesis or theme*-inscription of the *thesis*. But perhaps the debate between us, on this point, rests on a "verbal," "nominal" misunderstanding. And one can always redefine, beneath the same word (extraction, graft, extension), the concept of *position*.

2. It is true that in this case one would encounter the problem of the concept of the concept, and the problem of the relationship between the concept and the other.

As we cannot take this up here, I will say only this: if I ask to look closer, concerning this concept of position (and several others to which you link it), it is that it bears at least the same name as an *absolutely essential, vital* mechanism (even if sometimes unnoticed) of speculative Hegelian dialectics *(Setzung)*. (The position-of-the-other, in Hegelian dialectics, is always, finally, to pose-oneself by oneself as the other of the Idea, as other—than—oneself in one's finite determination, with the aim of repatriating and reappropriating oneself, of returning close to oneself in the infinite richness of one's determination, etc.).

Thus there are at least two concepts of the *position*.

Why not leave *open* the discussion of this question of the position, of the *positions* (taking a position: position (/negation)? position-*affirmation*? overturning/displacement? etc.).

I take my leave. Thank you both.

P.S. And if we gave to this exchange, for its (germinal) title, the word *positions*, whose polysemia is marked, moreover, in the letter *s*, the "disseminating" letter *par excellence*, as Mallarmé said? I will add, concerning *positions*: scenes, acts, figures of dissemination.

NOTES

Derrida's notes are indicated by his initials, J. D. The editor's notes of the original French edition are indicated by the abbreviation Ed. N. Translator's notes are indicated by the abbreviation T. N.

Implications

1. T. N. *De la grammatologie* (Paris: Editions de Minuit, 1967), and translated by Gayatri Spivak as *Of Grammatology* (Baltimore: The Johns Hopkins University Press, 1976). *L'écriture et la différence* (Paris: Seuil, 1967), and translated by Alan Bass as *Writing and Difference* (Chicago: University of Chicago Press, 1978).

2. T. N. *La voix et le phénomène* (Paris: Presses Universitaires de France, 1967), and translated by David Allison as *Speech and Phenomena* (Evanston: Northwestern University Press, 1973).

3. T. N. In my "Translator's Introduction" to *Writing and Difference* there is a discussion of how to read this passage on the mutual "insertability" of *Writing and Difference, Of Grammatology,* and *Speech and Phenomena.* See pp. x–xi.

4. T. N. *L'origine de la géometrie de Husserl, Traduction et Introduction* (Paris: Presses Universitaires de France, 1962), and translated by John P. Leavey as *Edmund Husserl's Origin of Geometry: An Introduction* (Stonybrook: Hays, 1978).

5. T. N. The epigraph reads: "A name on being mentioned reminds us of the Dresden Gallery and of our last visit there: we wander through the rooms, and stand before a picture of Tenier's which represents a picture gallery. When we consider that pictures of the latter would in turn portray pictures which on their part exhibited readable inscriptions and so forth . . ." Husserl, *Ideas,* trans. W. R. Boyce Gibson (New York: Macmillan, 1962), p. 270.

6. T. N. "Freud and the Scene of Writing" in *Writing and Difference.*

7. T. N. I have followed my practice of translating *être* by Being and

étant by being throughout this book. For the rationale behind this see *Writing and Difference*, "Translator's Introduction," p. xvii.

8. T. N. "Glossematics" is a term coined by the Copenhagen School of linguistics, discussed at length in the first part of *Of Grammatology*.

9. T. N. *Brisure*, a term used in *Of Grammatology*, is untranslatable. It combines the meanings of "breaking" and "joining."

10. T. N. I have followed my practice in *Writing and Difference* of leaving *différance* untranslated when it combines the two meanings about to be discussed.

11. T. N. "Structuralism" is often accused of ignoring historical, genetic considerations. Derrida often shows that this (justified) criticism of structuralism shares metaphysical presuppositions with structuralism. See "'Structure and Genesis' and Phenomenology" in *Writing and Difference*.

12. T. N. "Force and Signification" in *Writing and Difference*.

13. T. N. *Tel Quel* is the literary-theoretical journal, edited by Philippe Sollers et al., in which several of Derrida's major texts first appeared. See below, "Positions" note 28 for more on Derrida's relationship to *Tel Quel*.

14. T. N. This question is treated at length in *"La pharmacie de Platon"* in *La dissémination* (Paris: Seuil, 1972).

15. T. N. "Meaning" in French is conveyed both by *"sens"* and *"vouloir-dire." "Vouloir-dire"* is etymologically linked to the idea of will *(voluntas)*. It carries the connotation that meaning is the "will to say."

Semiology and Grammatology

1. J. D. That is, the intelligible. The difference between the signifier and the signified has always reproduced the difference between the sensible and the intelligible. And it does so no less in the twentieth century than in its stoic origins. "Modern structuralist thought has clearly established this: language is a system of signs, and linguistics is an integral part of the science of signs, *semiotics* (or to use Saussure's terms, *semiology*). The medieval definition—*aliquid stat pro aliquo*—resuscitated by our epoch has shown itself to be still valid and fruitful. Thereby, the constitutive mark of every sign in general, of the linguistic sign in particular, resides in its double character: every linguistic unity is bipartite, and comports two aspects: one sensible and the other intelligible—on the one hand, the *signans* (Saussure's *signifier*), and on the other, the *signatum* (the *signified*)." (Roman Jakobson, *Essais de linguistique générale* [Paris: Editions de Minuit, 1963], p. 162.)

2. Ed. N. See *De la grammatologie*, pp. 196–8.

3. T. N. In other words, *différance* combines and confuses "differing" and "deferring" in both their active and passive senses.

4. T. N. Edmund Husserl, *Ideas,* trans. W. R. Boyce Gibson (New York: Collier Books), p. 319.

5. Ed. N. See *De la grammatologie,* p. 12.

6. J. D. "But for now it suffices to remark that the foundation of my characteristic is also that of the demonstration of God's existence; for simple thoughts are the elements of the characteristic, and simple forms are the source of things. Now, I maintain that all simple forms are compatible with each other. This is a proposition whose demonstration I could not well give without explaining at length the foundations of the characteristic. But if it is granted, it follows that the nature of God, which encloses all simple forms taken absolutely, is possible. Now, we proved above that God is, provided that he is possible. Therefore, he exists. Q.E.D." (Letter to Princess Elizabeth, 1678.)

7. Ed. N. See *De la grammatologie,* pp. 83ff.

Positions

1. T. N. *Théorie d'ensemble* (Paris: Seuil, 1968). *"La différance"* is also in *Marges de la philosophie* (Paris: Editions de Minuit, 1972).

2. T. N. Houdebine, here, seems to be using *"relève"* in a technical sense that Derrida would *not* use in this context, as he says below in answer to Houdebine's first intervention. In the technical sense, *relève* is Derrida's translation of the Hegelian term *Aufhebung,* which means to preserve and to negate in a spiritual "lifting up" to a "higher level." Although the English "lifting up" has some relationship to *Aufhebung,* it is not an appropriate technical translation of the Hegelian term. Thus, throughout this interview, whenever *relève* is used in the technical sense I have left it untranslated.

3. T. N. *"La double séance"* (on Mallarmé) and *"La dissémination"* (on Sollers), reprinted in *La dissémination* (along with *"La pharmacie de Platon"* and *"Hors livre"*). *"La mythologie blanche"* in *Poétique* 5 (1971), and reprinted in *Marges.*

4. Ed. N. "It is proposed by a mute mark, by a tacit monument, I will say even by a pyramid, thinking not only of the form of the letter when printed as a capital, but of the text in Hegel's *Encyclopedia* in which the body of the sign is compared to the Egyptian pyramid." *"La différance,"* in *Théorie d'ensemble,* p. 42. (Reprinted in *Marges de la philosophie* [Paris: Les Editions de Minuit], p. 4.) This allusion is developed in a contemporary essay (*"Le puits et la pyramide, Introduction à la sémiologie de Hegel,* January 1968, in *Hegel et la pensée moderne* [Paris: Presses Universitaires de France], and reprinted in *Marges,* p. 79) in which the discourse of the *logos,* which draws the all-speaking truth from the bottom of a well, is opposed to the writing older than truth which is marked on the front of a monument.

5. Ed. N. See *"La double séance"* in *La dissémination.* (T. N. The French words left untranslated are all "homonyms," that is, they contain a variety of meanings beneath the same acoustic signifier. They "mean": "blank meaning," "white blood," "without blank," "one hundred blanks," "seeming." All the terms Derrida cites here function similarly: they combine several meanings—sometimes antithetical ones—beneath the same signifier. Such terms, Derrida always shows, are the only way to conceptualize writing in the sense of the "general text." In the history of philosophy, terms with double meanings are the ones that have been used to disqualify writing. For example, for Plato writing is a *pharmakon,* both remedy and poison. For Rousseau it is a *supplement,* both the missing and extra "piece" of language. All of these terms "inscribe" *différance* within themselves: they are always different from themselves, they always defer any singular grasp of their meaning. Thus it is not coincidence that philosophy has always, if blindly, used such terms to describe and disqualify writing.)

6. T. N. Derrida is playing on the word *foyer,* which is accurately translated by "focal point," but also means hearth, the point from which light emanates. This is what connects it to the crucible, in the laboratory sense. Like the French *foyer* and *creuset,* focal point and crucible are etymologically connected to ideas of luminousness and intersection.

7. Ed. N. *De la grammatologie,* p. 40, "From Restricted to General Economy" in *Writing and Difference,* and passim. (T. N. See also note 2 above.)

8. Ed. N. See also *"La différance,"* p. 58 (*Marges,* p. 20); "The Two Forms of Writing," "Writing and General Economy," "The Transgression of the Neutral and the Displacement of the *Aufhebung*" in *Writing and Difference* ("From Restricted to General Economy," pp. 262ff.); *"Ousia et grammē: Note sur une note de Sein und Zeit"* (in *Marges,* p. 31), on the "fissures" of the "metaphysical text": "two texts, two hands, two glances, two listening posts" . . . "the relationship between the two texts . . . can in no way yield to being read in the form of presence, supposing that something can ever yield to *reading* in this form" (pp. 256–57). Concerning the *"double register* in grammatological practice" and its relationship to science, see "Semiology and Grammatology" (interview with Julia Kristeva) above.

9. Ed. N. On *position* and *punctuality* see *"La parole soufflée"* in *Writing and Difference,* p. 194. On the critique of punctuality, see *Speech and Phenomena* and *"Ousia et grammē."* (I add: the signature is deviant, in and of itself. J. D.)

10. T. N. This untranslatable series functions similarly to the one discussed in note 5 above. All the terms play on the derivation of *écart* (literally the distance between two separate things) from the Latin

quartus. Thus the series literally reads: square, stature, card, chart, four. As in note 5 above, the etymological play is a simulated one: not all the words of the series actually derive from *quartus.*

11. T. N. As in notes 5 and 10 above, there is another simulated play on etymology here. The series in French is *marque, marge, marche.* *"Marche"* in French has the sense not only of "march," but also of "step," "degree," "action of movement by walking," etc. As noted above, this etymological play, whether simulated or real, serves as an inscription of "concepts" that simultaneously mean either or neither of their usual senses.

12. T. N. See note 2 above for the translation of *Aufhebung* by *relève.* *Erinnerung* is the "interiorizing memory" into which contradictions are "lifted up" (negated) and preserved.

13. J. D. "Difference in general is already contradiction in itself." (*"Der Unterschied überhaupt ist schon der Widerspruch an sich."* 11, 1, cg. 2 C) Since it can no longer simply be subsumed by the generality of *logical* contradiction, *différance* (the process of differentiation) permits a differentiated accounting for heterogeneous modes of conflictuality, or, if you will, for contradictions. If I have more often spoken of conflicts of force than of contradiction, this is first of all due to a critical wariness as concerns the Hegelian concept of contradiction *(Widerspruch)*, which, in addition, as its name indicates, is constructed in such a way as to permit its resolution within dialectical *discourse,* in the immanence of a concept capable of its own exteriority, capable of maintaining what is outside it right next to it. To reduce *différance* to difference is to stay far behind in this debate. Whose ellipsis is striking, for example, in this kind of formulation: "Scription contra-diction to reread" [*La dissémination*, pp. 182 and 403. Ed. N.]. Thus defined, the "undecidable," which is not contradiction in the Hegelian form of contradiction, situates, in a rigorously Freudian sense, the *unconscious* of philosophical contradiction, the unconscious which ignores contradiction to the extent that contradiction belongs to the logic of speech, discourse, consciousness, presence, truth, etc.

14. Ed. N. *"La différance,"* in *Marges,* p. 21. See also the discussion that followed, in *Bulletin de la Société française de philosophie.*

15. J. D. On the irreducibly *conflictual* character of *différance* and the *alterity* inscribed in it, see, among many other places, *"La différance,"* *Marges,* pp. 8, 21. Concerning the relationship to dialectics, see, for example, *Writing and Difference,* p. 248.

16. Ed. N. See *Writing and Difference,* passim. *"La différance"* and *"La mythologie blanche"* in *Marges,* pp. 11 and 247.

17. T. N. All further references to the Colloquium acts are in the text, and are indicated by page number.

18. J. D. I rejoice even more in that it appears (although I do not think

so at all) that the opposite already is thought in another quarter. I do not think so at all because to do so would be to keep watch over theoretical novelties as one watches the weather, that is, with an intention to inaugurate a season of theoretical prizes (which, after all, would represent a certain idea of what production and consummation *are worth* in this domain). In fact, this would amount to a vulgarly empiricist misconstruing of textual systematics, of the necessity, forms, and time of its development.

19. Ed. N. *De la grammatologie*, p. 142.

20. Ed. N. Among numerous other places, see the entire first part of *De la grammatologie*, passim. (For example: "The enigmatic model of the *line*, therefore, is that which philosophy could not see for as long as its eyes were open to the inside of its own history. This night begins to end somewhat when linearity—which is not the loss or the absence, but the suppression of multidimensional symbolic thought—loosens its oppression, because it has begun to sterilize the technical and scientific economy that it has long favored. In effect, its possibility has long been in structural solidarity with the possibility of economy, technology and ideology. This solidarity appears in the process of thesaurization, capitalization, sedentarization, hierarchization, and of the formation of ideology by the class of those who write, or rather who control the scribes." pp. 128–29. And notably from *"Ousia et grammē"*: "A writing exceeding everything that the history of metaphysics has included in the line, in its circle, in its time and its space.")

21. J. D. But it is true that I am very interested in the history of philosophy in its "relative autonomy." This is what appears indispensable to me: the theoretical critique is also a "discourse" (which is its specific form), and if it is to be articulated rigorously along with a more general practice, it has to take into account the most powerful *discursive* formation, the most powerful, extended, durable, and systematic formation of our "culture." This is the condition that permits us to avoid empiricist improvisation, false discoveries, etc., and that gives a systematic character to deconstruction.

22. J. D. On this point I permit myself to refer to *"La mythologie blanche"* (*Marges*, p. 275) and *Le puits et la pyramide"* (*Marges*, pp. 82–83).

23. J. D. See, notably, *De la grammatologie*, pp. 65ff., and "Semiology and Grammatology" [above].

24. J. D. I will be permitted to recall, here, that the first text I published concerned particularly the problem of writing as the condition of scientificity (Introduction to Husserl's *The Origin of Geometry*).

25. Ed. N. After the citation of a passage from Heidegger on *Fallen* and *Verfallen*: "Now, is not the opposition of the *originary* and the *derived* a properly metaphysical one? Is not the quest for the *archi-* in

general, whatever the precautions with which one surrounds this concept, the essential operation of metaphysics? Supposing that one could eliminate it from every other point of departure, despite many indications, is there not at least some element of Platonism in the *Verfallen*? Why determine as *fall* the passage from one temporality to another? And why qualify temporality as authentic—and proper *(eigentlich)*—and inauthentic—or improper—when every ethical preoccupatioon has been suspended? One could multiply these questions concerning the concept of finitude, the point of departure in the existential analytic of *Dasein*, justified by the enigmatic proximity to itself or identity with itself of the questioning (sec. 5), etc. If we have chosen to investigate the opposition which structures the concept of temporality, it is that the entire existential analytic leads back to it." ("*Ousia et grammē*" in *Marges*, pp. 73–74.)

26. Ed. N. *Marges*, pp. 251–57. And the entire development of note 7 in "*La double séance*" in *La dissémination*.

27. Ed. N. *Marges*, pp. 75ff.

28. T. N. Derrida is alluding to the following events. On 12 September 1969 *L'Humanité*, the newspaper of the French Communist Party, published an article by Jean Pierre Faye entitled "*Le Camarade Mallarmé*" ("Comrade Mallarmé"). Faye had been one of the editors of *Tel Quel*, until ideological differences led him to found his own journal, *Change*. Further, *Tel Quel* at the time was openly supporting the French Communist party. Without mentioning names, Faye attacked *Tel Quel*, alleging, among other things, that "a language, derived from Germany's extreme-right [in the period between the wars], has been *displaced*, unknown to all, and has been introduced into the Parisian left." A week later, Philippe Sollers, for *Tel Quel*, and Claude Prevost, a party intellectual, responded to Faye's attack, in letters published both in *L'Humanité* and *Tel Quel*. Both letters attacked Faye for confusing Heidegger with his Nazi interpreters, and accused him of defaming Derrida. Faye insisted upon a counter-response, published in *Tel Quel* 40, which was again counter-attacked, this time by the entire editorial board of *Tel Quel*.

The ironic sequel to these events is that in June 1971, *Tel Quel* broke with the Communist Party and declared itself Maoist. Eventually Sollers and *Tel Quel* attacked, and broke with, Derrida on political-theoretical grounds. June 1971 is also the date of this interview with Houdebine and Scarpetta, and the date might explain why Houdebine seems to press Derrida more and more, as the interview continues, on the question of Marxism. Houdebine seems to want Derrida to take a yes-or-no *position* on the compatibility of his work with dialectical materialism. Derrida always insists, as he says in the postscript of his letter to

Houdebine which concludes this text, on the metaphysical nature of taking a yes-or-no position, preferring the ambiguity of positions, whence the title of the interview.

This is not the place to pursue further the political history of Sollers and *Tel Quel*. Suffice it to say that neither is any longer Maoist or Communist.

29. J. D. Of the two communications to which I am referring here, the one from which I extract this last citation is not, despite numerous contradictions and uncertainties (to be ascribed to level of education), the more insufficient of the two, it seems to me. Honesty compels me to acknowledge this, and to avoid confusing the two.

30. J. D. See *"La différance," Marges*, p. 11.

31. J. D. An example: "If the word 'history' did not bear within itself the motif of a final repression of difference, one could say that only differences can be, from the outset and in all aspects, 'historical.' What is written as *différance* will indicate, then, the movement of play that 'produces,' in a way that is not simply an activity, these differences, these effects of difference. This does not mean that the *différance* which produces differences is before them, in a simple present that is itself unmodified, in-different. *Différance* is the nonfull, nonsimple 'origin,' the structured and differing origin of differences. The name 'origin,' therefore, is no longer suitable. . . . Retaining at least the schema, if not the content of the demand formulated by Saussure, we will designate as *différance* the movement according to which language, or any other code, any system of reference in general, is constituted 'historically' as a tissue of differences. 'Is constituted,' 'is produced,' 'is created,' 'movement,' 'historically,' etc., have to be understood beyond the metaphysical language in which they are caught, along with all their implications. We would have to show why the concepts of production, like those of constitution and of history, from this point of view remain in complicity with what is in question here, but this would take us too far today—in the direction of the representation of the 'circle' in which we appear to be enclosed—and I utilize them here, as I do many other concepts, only for strategic convenience and in order to undertake the deconstruction of their system at the point which is currently most decisive." Ibid., pp. 12–13. See also, for example, *"La double séance,"* in *La dissémination*, pp. 235–36. On the dissymmetry of this deconstruction, see especially notes 18 and 19.

32. J. D. In my improvised response, I had forgotten that Scarpetta's question also named *historicism*. Of course, the critique of historicism in all its forms seems to me indispensable. What I first learned about this critique in Husserl (from *Philosophy as a Rigorous Science* to the *Origin of*

Geometry: Hegel is always the target of this critique, whether directly or whether through Dilthey), who, to my knowledge, was the first to formulate it under this heading and from the point of view of theoretical and scientific (especially mathematical) rigor, seems valid to me in its argumentative framework, even if in the last analysis it is based on a historical teleology of truth. On this last question the issue is to be reopened. The issue would be: can one criticize historicism in the name of something other than *truth and science* (the value of universality, omnitemporality, the infinity of value, etc.), and what happens to science when the *metaphysical* value of *truth* has been put into question, etc.? How are the effects of science and of truth to be reinscribed? This brief reminder in order to mention that during the course of our interview Nietzsche's name was not pronounced. By chance? On what we are speaking about at this very moment, as on everything else, Nietzsche is for me, as you know, a very important reference. Finally, it goes without saying that in no case is it a question of a *discourse against truth* or against science. (This is impossible and absurd, as is every heated accusation on this subject.) And when one analyzes systematically the value of truth as *homoiosis* or *adequatio,* as the certitude of the *cogito* (Descartes, Husserl), or as a certitude opposed to truth in the horizon of absolute knowledge *(Phenomenology of the Mind),* or finally as *alētheia,* unveiling or presence (the Heideggerean repetition), it is not in order to return naively to a relativist or sceptical empiricism. (See, notably, *De la grammatologie,* p. 232, and *"La différance"* in *Marges,* p. 7.) I repeat, then, leaving all their disseminating powers to the proposition and the form of the verb: *we must have [il faut]* truth. For those who mystify (themselves) to have it trippingly on the tongue. Such is the law. Paraphrasing Freud, speaking of the present/absent penis (but it is the same thing), we must recognize in truth "the normal prototype of the fetish." How can we do without it?

33. T. N. See "From Restricted to General Economy: A Hegelianism Without Reserve" in *Writing and Difference.*

34. J. D. To summarize that which marks it within the deconstructed field, again I will cite Nietzsche: "Let us renounce the notions of 'subject' and 'object,' and then the notion of 'substance,' and consequently all of its diverse modifications, for example, 'matter,' 'spirit,' and the other hypothetical beings, 'eternity,' and the 'immutability of matter,' etc. Thus we also get rid of materiality." I also refer to his *Unzeitgemasse . . . ,* 2.

35. J. D. Here I permit myself to recall that the texts to which you have referred (particularly *"La double séance," "La dissémination," "La mythologie blanche,"* but also *"La pharmacie de Platon"* and several

others) are situated *explicitly* in relation to Bataille, and also explicitly propose a reading of Bataille.

36. J. D. On this subject, and notably on the paradoxes of dissymmetry and alterity, see for example "Violence and Metaphysics" in *Writing and Difference*.

37. J. D. Nor is the heterogeneity of "matter" to be constituted as transcendence, whether the transcendence of the Law, the Great Exterior Object (constitutive and consoling severity of the paternal agency), or of the (appeasing and/or cruel) Element of the mother (see what Freud says about the well-known relationship mother/matter in the passage in which he makes evident that which *cannot be reduced* to the variation of *linguistic*, verbal signifiers. See lecture 10 of the *Introductory Lectures on Psychoanalysis*, and also the end of "Freud and the Scene of Writing" in *Writing and Difference*). This does not imply that matter has no necessary relationship to these agencies, but rather that the relationship is one of written concatenation, a play of substitution of differential marks that relate matter also to writing, to the remainder, to death, to the phallus, to excrement, to the infant, to semen, etc., or at least to everything in this that is not subject to the *relève*. And requires, thus, that this relationship not be made either into a new essential determination of the Being of beings, the center of a new ontology, or into a new example of the *master-words*, which Marx, for example, definitively criticized in the *German Ideology*.

38. J. D. See *La dissémination*, pp. 203–9 and 253.

39. J. D. Beside the reading of Benveniste's analyses that I cited in "*La double séance*," the works and teaching of H. Wismann and J. Bollack also have guided me on this terrain. In the course of a seminar at the *École normale* I attempted to investigate the text of the *Timaeus* from this point of view, especially the very problematical notion of the *chora*.

40. T. N. See *Writing and Difference*, pp. 246–48.

41. J. D. See "*La mythologie blanche*" in *Marges*, p. 255.

42. J. D. In rereading this passage of our interview, I perceive that by specifying "not only linguistic" (this is only a reminder of what I reiterate without respite), in principle I answered the ensemble of your question, which presupposed explicitly that differences are "linguistic differences, types of linguistic signifiers."

I specify again that spacing is a concept which also, but not exclusively, carries the meaning of a productive, positive, generative force. Like *dissemination*, like *différance* it carries along with it a *genetic* motif: it is not only the interval, the space constituted between two things (which is the usual sense of spacing), but also spac*ing*, the operation, or in any event, the movement of setting aside. This movement is inseparable from temporization-temporalization (see *"La différance"*) and from *différance*, from the conflicts of force at work in them. It marks what is set aside from itself, what interrupts every self-identity, every punctual assemblage of the self, every self-homogeneity, self-interiority. (See *La voix et le phénomène*, p. 96.) This is why it was difficult for me to see—is still difficult for me to see—how, why you insisted upon separating it, to put it briefly, from the motif of the *eteron*. Certainly these two motifs do not absolutely overlap, but no concept overlaps any other concept—this is the law of spacing. Of course, if I had only endlessly repeated the unique word *spacing*, you would be completely right. But I have no less insisted on the *other* and on several others. Spacing also signifies, precisely, the impossibility of reducing the chain to one of its links or of absolutely privileging one—or the other. Finally, I must recall that *différance*, above all, is not a substance, an essence, a cause, etc. that could yield some "phenomenal deviation."

43. Ed. N. See, for example, *De la grammatologie*, chap. 1 (*"Le programme," "Le signifiant et la vérité," "L'être écrit"*), notably p. 32 n. 9; "Semiology and Grammatology" [above], and *"La double séance," La dissémination*, p. 284.

44. J. D. Your question on "what Lacan calls the symbolic" invites a thorough answer, an explanation of principles, if not, although this is not the place for it, a detailed explanation. Having for the first time accepted the law of the interview and the declarative mode, I will not be evasive. On the other hand I know that certain of my friends, for sometimes contradictory reasons, have regretted my neutrality on this subject. Hence the following, schematically.

In the texts that I have published so far, the absence of references to Lacan, in effect, is almost total. This is justified not only by the aggressions in the form of, or with the aim of, reappropriation that Lacan, since the appearance of *De la grammatologie* in *Critique* (1965) (and even earlier, I am told), has proliferated, whether directly or indirectly, in private or in public, in his seminars, and, from 1965 on, as I was to notice myself reading them, in almost *each* of his writings. Such movements corresponded, each time, to the argumentative framework precisely analyzed by Freud (*Interpretation of Dreams*) which I showed (*Grammatologie, "Pharmacie de Platon," "Le puits et la pyramide"*) always informs the traditional proceedings against writing. This is the so called "kettle" argument, which meets the needs of a cause by accumulating incompatible assertions. (1. Devaluation and rejection: "it is worthless" or "I do not agree." 2. Valuation and reappropriation: "moreover it is mine and I have always said so.") This constriction of discourse—which I regret—was not insignificant, and, here too, called for silent listening.

Perhaps I would not have maintained this silence if I had not felt justified, in addition, for reasons of a historico-theoretical nature (differing from the minor case of which we were speaking above).

A brief reminder then.

At the time of my first publications Lacan's *Écrits* had not been collected and published. When *De la grammatologie* and "*Freud et la scène de l'écriture*" were published I had read only "*Fonction et champ de la parole et du langage en psychanalyse*" and "*L'instance de la lettre dans l'inconscient ou la raison depuis Freud*" (cited in "*La parole soufflée*"). Assured of the importance of this problematic in the field of psychoanalysis, I will point out a certain number of major motifs that kept it within the critical questions that I was in the process of formulating, and *inside* the logocentric, that is phonologistic, field that I undertook to delimit and to shake. Among others these motifs were the following:

1. A telos of "full speech" in its essential tie (and sometimes effects of incantatory identification) to Truth. Here the chapter on "Empty and Full Speech in the Psychoanalytic Realization of the Subject" is to be reread in all the amplitude of its resonances: "Let us be categorical, in psychoanalytic anamnesis it is not a question of reality, but of truth, because the effect of full speech is to reorder past contingencies by giving them the meaning of necessities to come, such as they are constituted by the small amount of liberty in which the subject makes them present." (*Écrits* [Paris: Seuil, 1966], p. 256.) Also *so many other* propositions of this type: "the birth of truth in speech," "the truth of this revolution" in "present speech" (ibid.). Despite many elliptical and rhapsodic variations, since then I have never encountered any rigorous questioning of this value of truth in its most pertinent historical and architectonic site.

Now this critical questioning, precisely as it concerns the ties of full speech, truth, and presence (see, among other places, *De la grammatologie*, p. 18) is what I was then undertaking explicitly.

2. Under the heading of a return to Freud, a massive recourse to Hegelian conceptuality (more precisely, to the conceptuality of the *Phenomenology of the Mind* in the style of the period, and with no articulation to the system of the *Logic* or to Hegelian "semiology") and to the Heideggerean conceptuality (to *alētheia*, precisely, always defined as "revelation," "veiling/unveiling"; to the presence and the Being of beings, to *Dasein* once more become a subject! [p. 318]). I would be the last to consider this a regression *in itself*, but the absence of any theoretical and systematic explanation of the status of these importations (and of several others) sometimes seemed to me to derive, shall we say, from the philosophical facileness condemned at the end of

"L'instance de la lettre dans l'inconscient" and, echoing Freud, in *Scilicet I*. To state later that such motivic borrowings from the *Phenomenology of the Mind* were "didactic," or that the so frequently invoked vocabulary of transcendental phenomenology and of Husserlian idealism ("intersubjectivity," for example) was to be understood with an *"epochē"* [phenomenological reduction], and then to resolve such problems in a phrase seems to me rather slight.

Now, in my teaching and publications of the time, I was investigating explicitly, from the critical point of view with which you are familiar, the textual systematics of Hegel, Husserl, and Heidegger. In measuring the contortions of their proceedings, I understood that they could not be amalgamated in this way. No more could Freud.

3. A light-handed reference to the authority of phonology, and more precisely to Saussurian linguistics. This is Lacan's most specific work: on the basis of the Saussurian sign, and on it. With the implications and consequences you understand, writing is thus led back to the system of hearing oneself speak, to the point of idealizing the auto-affection in which it is interiorized, "lifted up" by the voice, corresponding to it, present in it, phoneticizing itself in it, being "always... *phonomatic,* and phonetic as soon as it is read" (*Écrits*, p. 470).

Now, I was in the process of elaborating a battery of critical questions on this subject, including the effects of phonologism in the psychoanalytic field, and the complexity of Freudian science in this respect ("Freud and the Scene of Writing").

4. An attention to the letter and to the written according to Freud, certainly, but without any specific investigation concerning the concept of writing, such as I was then attempting to delineate it, or concerning the oppositions and conflicts that then would have to be deciphered. I will come back in an instant to the decisive problem of "literature."

I am skipping over the connotations of Lacan's discourse and numerous indications of a reinstallation of the "signifier," and psychoanalysis in general, in a new metaphysics (whatever interest this might have in itself), in the space of what I then was delineating under the name of logocentrism, and singularly of phonocentrism. I am also skipping over numerous traits, which seemed to me, certainly in a complex and sometimes contradictory way, to anchor Lacan's enterprise in the postwar philosophical situation. (And much will have to be reread from this point of view. Follow too, the words "Being," "authentic," "true," "full.") It would be absurd to see in this a contingent or personal limitation, and, once more, the historical necessity is incontestable. It is simply that at the time of which I am speaking, I—and certain others with me—perceived other pressing questions. Finally I am skipping over the rhetoric, Lacan's style: its sometimes remarkable, and also sometimes anachronistic (I do not say untimely) effects (in relation to a certain advance and to a certain "program" of the times) seemed to me to be governed by the delay of a scene, conferring upon it, as I do not doubt, a certain necessity. (I am designating whatever constrained him to deal with institutionalized psychoanalysis in a certain way: this is Lacan's argument.) In relation to the theoretical difficulties that interested me, I read this style, above all, as an art of evasion. The vivacity of ellipsis too often seemed to me to serve as an avoidance or an envelopment of diverse problems. (The most significant example has since been provided by the clever "homonymic" feint by means of which the historico-theoretical difficulty of the determination of truth as *adaequatio rei et intellectus* is submerged. This determination of truth governs the entire discourse on "The Freudian Thing," and one must wonder, in the absence of an explanation, what organization allows it to coexist with truth as revelation—that is, presence—which itself organizes all the *Écrits*.) I recognize that this supposes as much lucidity in the determination of the difficulties as in the determination of the *dangers*. Perhaps this is a necessary moment in the preparation of a new problematic, provided that the evasion does not speculate too much, and that one not allow oneself to be captivated by the sumptuous representation of the procession and the parade.

Even if these reservations are far from exhausting Lacan's work, of which I remain persuaded, they were already important enough for me not to seek references (in the form of a guarantee) in a discourse so different, in its mode of elocution, its site, its aims, its presuppositions, from the texts that I was proposing. Such references would only result in the accumulation of fog in a field already not lacking it. They also risked compromising the possibility of a rigorous juxtaposition that perhaps remained to be constructed.

Was it necessary, then, on the contrary, to declare a disagreement from the outset and to engage an explicit debate? Aside from the fact that the grid of this debate seemed to me published in its premises (available for whomever was willing to read it and take it on), such a declaration did not seem opportune to me, at that time, for several reasons.

1. The ensemble of the *Écrits* having been published in the interval, I not only had to acquaint myself with it, but also to engage myself, given what I have just said about Lacan's rhetoric, in a labor that announced itself as out of proportion with what my initial readings had led me to expect. (I read while writing: slowly, taking pleasure in long prefaces to each term.) This certainly is not sufficient to make me give

up—I might have anticipated poorly—but perhaps to make me prefer to
respond for a time (I am speaking of a rather short lapse, three or four
years) to demands that I considered more urgent, and, in any event,
prerequisite.

2. If I had objections to formulate (but the debate does not necessarily
take the form of a disagreement; it can yield a more complex dis-
implication or displacement), I already knew that my objections would
have nothing in common with the ones current then. Here again, I held
to an avoidance of confusion, and to doing nothing to limit the pro-
pagation of a discourse whose critical effects seemed to me, despite
what I have just recalled, necessary within an entire field. (This is why,
I confirm in passing, I did what depended upon me to prevent the
interruption of Lacan's teaching at the *École normale*.) Here I refer to
what I have said elsewhere about insistence, intervals, and inequalities
of development.

3. *In this interval* I judged that the best contribution or theoretical
"explanation" consisted in pursuing my own work according to its
specific pathways and requirements, whether or not this work should
encounter Lacan's, and Lacan's—I do not at all reject the idea—more
than any other today.

Since then? Since then I have reread these two texts, and have read
others, almost all of them, I believe, in the *Écrits*. These last few months
notably. My first reading of them has been largely confirmed. Particularly, to come back to a point whose major importance you will recognize, as concerns the identification of truth (as unveiling) and speech
(logos). Truth—separated from knowledge—is constantly determined as
revelation, nonveiling, that is, necessarily, as presence, the presentation
of the present, the "Being of beings" *(Anwesenheit)* or, in an even more
literally Heideggerean fashion, as the unity of veiling and unveiling.
The references to the result of Heideggerean procedures are often explicit in this form ("the radical ambiguity indicated by Heidegger to the
extent that truth signifies revelation" [p. 166], "the passion for unveiling which has an object: the truth" [p. 193], etc.). That the ultimate signified of this speech or *logos* is posed as a *lack* (nonbeing, absent, etc.)
in no way changes this *continuum,* and moreover remains strictly
Heideggerean. And if, in effect, one needs to recall that there is no
metalanguage (I would say, rather, that there is nothing outside the
text, outside a certain angle of the remark [*Grammatologie*, p. 227, pas-
sim]), it must not be forgotten that the most classical metaphysics and
onto-theology can quite well accommodate metalanguage, especially
when the proposition takes the form of "Myself, the truth, I speak" or
"This is even why the unconscious, which says it, the truth on the

truth, is structured like a language..." (pp. 867–68). Above all I would
not say that this is *false*. I only repeat that the questions I have asked
bear on the necessity and presuppositions of this continuum.

And then I became quite interested in the "Seminar on 'The Purloined
Letter.'" An admirable achievement, and I do not say this conventionally, but one which seems to me, in its flight to find the "illustration" of a "truth" (p. 12), to misconstrue the map [*carte*], the functioning or fictioning, of Poe's text, of this text and its links to others, let
us say the *squaring* [*carrure*] of a scene of writing played out in it. [On
the play on *carte* and *carrure* see note 10 above. T. N.] Lacan's discourse, no more than any other, is not totally closed to this square, or to
its figure, which does not equal or unveil any speaking truth. This is
the heterogeneity of which I spoke at the beginning. It is not a question
of giving signs of this heterogeneity, of being open or closed to it, of
speaking of it much or little, but of knowing how, and up to what
point, to administer the scene and the chain of consequences. A pro-
foundly traditional reading of Poe's text then, a reading that is ultimately hermeneutic (semantic) *and* formalist (according to the schema
criticized in "*La double séance*," and that we summarized above). This is
what I will try to demonstrate, although I cannot do so here, by means
of the patient analysis of these two texts, which will take place, when I
have the time, in a work in preparation. [The work has since appeared.
See "*Le facteur de la verité*" in *Poetique* 21; translated as "The Purveyor
of Truth" in *Yale French Studies* 52. T. N.] Although it is doubtless productive in other respects, this misconstruing seems to me to be determined systematically by the limits I mentioned a moment ago under
the rubric of logocentrism (logos, full speech, "true speech," truth as the
oppostion veil/nonveil, etc.). Perhaps it is not essentially the misconstruing of the "literary" (although, from my point of view, this is a
fruitful test, particularly in the deciphering of Lacanian discourse), and
it is not a question here, once again, of preserving literature from the
grasp of psychoanalysis. I would even say the contrary. What is at
stake, what is in question, is a certain turn of writing which in effect is
often indicated under the heading of "literature" or "art," but which
can be defined only from the vantage of a *general* deconstruction which
resists against (or against which resists) not *psychoanalysis in general* (on
the contrary), but a certain capacity, a certain determined pertinence of
psychoanalytic concepts that can be measured here, at a certain stage of
their development. From this point of view, certain "literary" texts have
an "analytic" and deconstructive capacity greater than certain
psychoanalytic discourses which *apply* their theoretical apparatus to
these texts, or "apply" a given state of their theoretical apparatus, with
its openings, but also with its presuppositions, at a given moment of its

elaboration. Such would be the relationship between the theoretical apparatus supporting the "Seminar on 'The Purloined Letter'" (you know what a central role Lacan gives to it, at the entry to the *Écrits*), Poe's text, and doubtless several others.

This is where I am today. I deliver this note to the diverse movements whose program, henceforth, is more or less known.

45. T. N. What I have translated as "disem*bed*" is *se deliter*. This is a "clinical" play on words because both *deliter* and *clinique* derive from words meaning "bed," the French *lit* and the Greek *klinē*.

46. J. D. Have I not here indicated the principles of an answer—according to what you named earlier a certain *star*—to your last question?

In a word, I will also point out that except by taking into account what dissemination figures in this way, one is led necessarily to make the "symbolic" and the tripartition imaginary/symbolic/real into an unmodifiable transcendental or ontological structure (see on this subject, *De la grammatologie*, p. 90).

These questions relative to psychoanalysis are *de facto* and *de jure* indissociable—as psychoanalysts often say—from analytic "experience" and "practice," and therefore also—and psychoanalysts insist on this rarely—from the historical, political, and economic conditions for this practice. As concerns some "kernel" of the "analytic situation," it seems to me that there is no final, inviolate protocol absolutely given as guaranteed by "science." And the condemnation of American psychoanalysis, however justified, should not serve as a too effective distraction. This is a very complex question, but its givens will submit to an ineluctable historical transformation.

47. T. N. The phrase in French is: *"la dissémination figure ce qui* ne revient pas *au père." Revenir à* means come back to, fall to (as an inheritance) and amount to. These multiple meanings—weakly translated as that which *cannot be* the father's—lapidarily figure Derrida's critique of Lacan in *"Le facteur de la verité."* If germination ("semen") and castration ("phallus")—roughly the signified and the signifier—are expressions of what the father must lose with no possibility of return, then Lacan's idea that the phallus-signifier-letter always arrives at its destination, comes back to where it should be, repeats the metaphysical gesture of confining the "letter" to a trajectory governed by the laws of return to a *true* origin.

48. T. N. As in note 47 above, this prefigures the critique of Lacan in *"Le facteur de la verité."* For reasons related to those just given above, Derrida finally states that in the "Seminar on 'The Purloined Letter'" the phallus-letter is made to function as a transcendental signifier, that is, as the signifier of a true, original absence.

49. J. D. *La dissémination*, p. 336.

50. J. D. *"La double séance"* in *La dissémination*, p. 293.

51. T. N. Freud's text on *The Uncanny* ("*Das Unheimliche*") was written at about the same time as *Beyond the Pleasure Principle* (1919), and is in many ways related to the latter. Derrida has made much of this connection.

52. Ed. N. "The 'subject' of writing does not exist if we mean by that some sovereign solitude of the author. The subject of writing is a *system* of relations between strata: the Mystic Pad, the psyche, society, the world. Within that scene, on that stage, the punctual simplicity of the classical subject is not to be found." "Freud and the Scene of Writing," in *Writing and Difference*, p. 227.

53. J. D. The discussion was published in the *Bulletin de la société française de philosophie* (January 1968).

54. T. N. As the citation in note 52 above indicates, much of this discussion relates to "Freud and the Scene of Writing" in which Derrida analyzes Freud's text on the mystic writing pad, called the *bloc magique* (*Wunderblock*) in French. The "block" of the general text refers to the deconstruction of all inherited concepts, in all fields (psychoanalysis, literary criticism, anthropology, sociology, linguistics, philosophy, etc.) in terms of the problematic of writing. In the "Note on the Mystic Writing Pad" (1925), Freud comes to conceive of the entire psyche in scriptural terms.

55. Ed. N. "What we know of these exchanges is accessible only through language and the text, in the infrastructural sense that we now attribute to this word." *De la grammatologie*, p. 234.

56. Ed. N. On the critique of the *philosophical* idea of the *region*, and the *ontological* opposition of the *regional* and the *nonregional*, see *De la grammatologie*, p. 35.